Designing Woman

DESIGNING WOMAN

*The art and practice of
theatrical costume design
by Virginia Volland*

Doubleday & Company, Inc., Garden City, New York, 1966

Library of Congress Catalog Card Number 66–11056
Copyright © 1966 by Virginia Volland
All Rights Reserved
Printed in the United States of America
First Edition

Dedication

*To the Actors' Fund, for its great assistance,
and to those friends from New York to California
without whose help and understanding
I would never have been able to work out
a new design for living.*

Foreword

I began my working years as an actress.

For reasons that eluded me at the time, but that show up very clearly if you have twenty-twenty hindsight, I was not a great success as a member of Actors' Equity. But I had a few jobs, and spent three years at it after I came to New York, and I did get hired as a member of the company for the first season of the brand-new Westport Country Playhouse. It was fun, with Dorothy Gish, and Peggy Wood, and some others you probably never heard of. . . .

One day I turned up at rehearsal in one of those simple little cottons calculated to withstand Westport heat, and Dorothy asked me where on earth I had gotten that dear dress? "Made it," said I, a bit ashamed it wasn't something I had picked up at Best and Co. I hadn't even heard of Berg-dorf Goodman in those days. "Could you, would you, make me one just like it?" Flattered no end, I did, and I remem-

ber charging her eleven dollars for it—six was for the fabric
and five, as I learned later to say, for the needle.

The first dress I ever made for anyone other than myself.
The first dress I ever got money for. The first dress I ever
made for an *actress*.

It was almost twenty years later that I began designing for
Broadway seriously and professionally. But I know now, that
was the dress, that was the day that did it.

Before I became a member of USA I made dresses for Bea
Lillie, Mrs. Richard Rodgers, Blanche Yurka, Mildred Dunnock, costumes for Lloyd Bridges and Alex Scourby, dressed
Jack Cole's dancers for nightclub engagements. But that was
the day and the dress. That day—I was hooked.

I hope that some of you who read this will become theatrical costume designers, with the help of this book.

I hope, just as fervently, that some of you will not, also
aided and abetted by what you will read here.

There is more involved in successful costume designing for
the theatre, or TV, or the movies, than the ability to create
a handsome sketch of a chic dress or a magnificent toga. It
is a whole different world from the one you will inhabit in
your own couturier salon or working for a Seventh Avenue
manufacturer, if you are to cross swords with Broadway on a
full-time basis. And if you are not to be successful at it, it's a
lean and hungry world as well. Even the man who makes a
go of this profession has to tighten his belt at times. So, if
you aren't making a go, you can get to where tightening that
belt isn't enough—you may have to eat it. It is to avoid these
failures that it is worthwhile to look closely at the nongraphic,
as well as at the more tactile, requirements for the part.

I say part because to dress an actor, you must have something of the actor in you. You have to be part ham, at least, to hang around the theatre as much as will be demanded of you. To put it simply, you have to have the temperament. Since this is in no sense a story of suspense, I am about to break one of the primary rules and suggest that you take a look right now at the last chapter before you go on or rush out to take a course in designing or wear out your shoe leather and enthusiasm. You have a right to know the end of the story. Then, if you are not too discouraged, come back and start with Chapter 1.

Contents

Designing Woman

1

How to Get That First Job

No one can tell you how to get it.

There isn't any accepted method of procedure.

To begin with, there are no employment agencies in this field, although Lord knows there should be. Neither are there agents or talent representatives as there are for actors and playwrights. No, you are strictly on your own and there will be times when this position may seem to you to be unwarrantedly isolated.

As a matter of fact, your union, the Theatrical Costumer's Union, United Scenic Artists, Local 829, which you must join before you are allowed to design costumes for Broadway (*see* Chapter 2 for details), comes as close as anything to being an employment agency for costume designers. Most producers call the union to locate the designer they want, so be sure that United Scenic Artists is kept *au courant* as to your address and telephone number if you are expecting any calls. Like the medical associations and the ethics that rule out specific recommendations of doctors' names, I do not believe that Local 829 ever suggests a specific name of a designer, but then neither do I think they are often asked. Such recommendations have to be put into producers' minds by somebody else and that's what we're going to talk about here.

In fact it is a good idea to hang around your union for a while even if as a new member you may feel a little strange. The union is your best shopping center for a job. So go to all the union meetings. This is where you will meet the scene designers who are the superior and ranking members of 829. Not all of them go to meetings, but there will be enough present as a rule to make it interesting. These are other people who can help you find work since often a producer will ask the scene designer whom he would recommend on the clothes front. The scenic artist has usually been hired well in advance of many other people who will be employed by the production simply because it takes so long to construct the sets. If the costumer can, in his own tactful fashion, so convince a set designer of his, the costumer's, genius, that he will put in a request for him or suggest his name to other people, it is easy to see how helpful all this can be. If this advice sounds as if the costumer must cringe like a fawning toady, I can only say that it all depends on how you do it. If you genuinely like and admire someone's work and ability and can communicate this without sounding like Da Vinci in search of a patron, it is quite possible that the admired may learn to like you. But be sure to pick someone for whom your respect and admiration are genuine or you may have to eat the false words someday. You are establishing in these beginnings not only your reputation as a creative worker but your standards of taste.

All of this may sound like an attempt to revive the old cliché about job-hunting: it isn't what you know that gets you a job, it's who you know. It is a cliché because it is so true as to be a platitude. Theatre people tend to band together in certain respects against the outside world. To be considered, recommendations must come from professionals in the theatre field. The only thing the really nontheatrical businessman can contribute that will be accepted cheerfully is money. This man can only figure in casting to the extent of casting himself as an angel. A producer getting ready to launch a new play may very well call up a friend of his who is head of a soft drinks corporation and invite him to the audition of a new play. But when the friend asks if he can contribute anything to the evening, the producer never suggests he bring along that ravishing blonde he's been seen with around town, she looks like the type they want for a leading lady. He says, "Sure, Joe. Bring money."

This is the reason your best friends for job-hunting purposes are not the money-minded but the creative people with theatrical talent. Never turn down an invitation to meet a producer, set designer, author, or actor or actress. Next to set designers the latter are the most useful. You never can tell when they will land a job where they will be in a position to ask for their own favorite designer.

Conversely, the author is the least useful to the costumer. His area is mainly in the field of acting as far as the production is concerned and actually, according to the terms of a Dramatists' Guild contract, he really only has the power of veto. He may not be able to promote his favorite actor but he can make things damned uncomfortable for a nonfavorite. Read *The Seesaw Log* by Mr. Gibson.

I got my first Broadway job by a fluke. For years I had been friends with Polly Rowles, an actress for whom I had made clothes for a personal wardrobe, and one day she gave me a script she was considering for fall production. She knew I was so interested in the theatre that I read every original play I could get my hands on. When I gave it back to her I said, "Very funny; I like it."

"Do you?" she said in surprise. "I feel very dubious about the whole thing . . ."

"I'm so sure it's going to be a hit I'd give a pretty to do the clothes!" I replied with my usual vehemence. And I realized I was speaking the truth.

My friend still sounded doubtful. "Would you really? Well, I'll tell the producer if I ever see him. I may just send the play back with no comment."

But she did the play, *Time Out for Ginger,* and so did I, and the ice was broken for me when the play ran a year and then went out on tour for almost the same length of time.

Off-Broadway, amateur, and summer theatres are often good lead-ins to the Main Stem. These places are easier for the novice to crash and may be a source of many good contacts. Many professional theatre people will work at these levels for the opportunity to keep busy or to work on something they believe in that they could not do any other way, such as acting a certain part or directing a so-far-undiscovered play. So job-hunt in these areas even if the financial returns are small or nonexistent. It is a worthwhile gamble if you can manage to eat while you watch the tote board. Quite a long time ago there was an organization called the Comedy Club, which was strictly amateur except for the fact that it hired professional directors for its two plays a year. I was persuaded to design the costumes strictly for free. The director of one of these plays was Ruth Rawson. When a year or so later I was asked to estimate for a play on Broadway for which I did not know the producer or anyone in the organization, or so I thought, I found that Ruth was directing and had suggested me.

Another reason for investing time and effort in this kind of work is that it helps the designer pile up credits on his dossier at a time when it is much better to have done something than not to have any credits. If you are worried as to whether these groups can afford that union salary of yours, don't. Call United Scenic Artists and you will find that they have different rates for different categories of theatres. The thing to worry about is yourself. Can you afford to work on an empty stomach?

Many years ago, before I was even a member of the union, I worked my fingers to the bone and myself into a state of somnambulistic euphoria doing costumes for a downtown theatre called the Playroom Club. The reason this operation was somnambulistic was that I already had another job, non-theatrical but full time. Other believers in this early cause were Mildred Dunnock, Alexander Scourby, and Lloyd Bridges, all as unknown as myself in those days. No money at all, but now one of the things on my dossier of which I am most proud is that work for what turned out to be the first theatre-in-the-round in New York, and the fact that I designed costumes for the first American production of Jean Cocteau's *Infernal Machine*. The costumes got a favorable review in *Daily Variety* (the California edition), and since then several college theatres that were doing the play have written me asking for permission to borrow my sketches and duplicate my designs.

Another gambit not without its uses is to take a job as assistant to an already established costumer. This will pay enough to live on with a tight belt and may produce valuable contacts and experience. You may find you are functioning chiefly as an errand boy, but this has the advantage, as you go from jewelry resource to fabric center, of helping you build up your collection of Important Trivia so necessary to your own future jobs.

Many producers, at least the ones who are human, respond to the siren call of "I can get it for you wholesale." Knowing this, I once prepared a campaign in advance. I had for a time worked on Seventh Avenue and I had a few contacts. I also had a friend who was a better-dress buyer and she did some groundwork for me. For the rest, I had a certain amount of brass of my own. I went around to these people to ask which of them would be willing to provide merchandise at wholesale prices for a Broadway production in return for credit in the program, and eventually I lined up a list of women's wardrobe suppliers from coats to shoes to dresses to costume jewelry. This is not as simple as one might think. It is very disrupting to the business of Seventh Avenue to turn the place over to a handful of actresses who see no reason why shopping at 530 Seventh Avenue should be any different from shopping at Bonwit's. They want to try everything on, whether it is applicable or not, and that is not *de rigueur* in wholesale. Then they start redesigning the line and would like this dress just fine if it had a different skirt, long sleeves, and were made in an entirely different fabric. . . . Well, you may not know about that yet so don't worry until it happens—with you in the middle!

Having lined up my treasures I had to wait to open this Pandora's box until I had an opportunity. But it came when a business manager I talked to was, I knew, considering two other costumers. The offer to save him all this money on the wardrobe put me head and shoulders above my competition. He was, after all, a real "moneyman" and I could offer him the thing he wanted.

The one thing a designer can do to get employment is to offer his services wholesale or cut-rate. The union frowns on this and is so serious about its displeasure that it is very likely to inflict exile as its punishment. Since your recompense for all these jobs is paid into the union, who in turn pays the designer, it is hard to fool the union.

I was once disciplined for what was a sincerely honest mistake. I simply counted the number of costumes wrong. Local 829 counted correctly, charged my producer that much more, and then fined me the extra amount they had collected, plus an additional two hundred and fifty dollars as a mild sort of reprimand. . . . So, as you can see, it's hardly worthwhile.

This list of entries to the theatre is not infallible, nor is it by any means complete. It is only meant to start you thinking. One good way to start is to make either clothes or costumes for people who are newsworthy and whose wardrobes are apt to be mentioned in the columns. I mean nightclub singers, dancers, or someone so chic and socially prominent that what she wears is cause for comment. Nancy Kelly, for instance, would do nicely.

There are a few things *not* to do. When I was a girl there was a current joke about actresses fainting on a producer's doorstep to attract his attention. Well, one year I was in California and I was very anxious to meet the head of Western Costume Company. I had heard that he was a very nice man and that he was looking for an assistant. I was sure that I was just what he would want if he could meet me and I pulled all kinds of wires until I got an appointment with Al Nickel.

The day arrived. Coiffed, wearing my best clothes, and supercharged with nervous tension, I departed for his office. I left in plenty of time but even then parking was a problem, to say the least. When I finally managed to abandon my car and rush into the building I was within minutes of being late.

Western Costume was in an old building peculiarly constructed. There was an anteroom to Mr. Nickel's office where his secretary sat and a door, closed, off to the right, that led to his private office. Just on the other side of that door, in fact flush with it, were two steps that adjusted the levels of the old buildings.

Perhaps it was being late or overeager, but I did not hear the secretary's warning. I opened the door and literally fell, full length—which is quite a lot of length—into the office of the man I wanted so much to impress.

He was terribly nice; but the pain was so great that, to my shame, I couldn't help crying. Mr. Nickel offered me his handkerchief, iodine, and alcohol, to be applied wherever they would do the most good. My hair, which was long and required time and many hairpins, was falling—my dress was torn, my stockings full of runs, and my legs so scratched as to be bleeding in several places. When I was finally restored enough to go on a tour of inspection that was part of the program, I had a limp of major proportions and occasionally emitted yips of pain. That costume company literally covered blocks. . . .

When I got home and could see a doctor I was ordered to bed for a week. I had sprained or wrenched something. And Mr. Nickel, although he was most charming and arranged other contacts for me, never gave me that luscious job. So, you see, never faint on a producer's doorstep. It might just make him think that you are apt to be unstable. . . .

2

How to Get Your Citizenship in the USA

A major portion of this book concerns itself with imagination, temperament, and the world of illusion. But now let's talk about some of the more stable elements. You cannot design for Broadway unless you are a member of the union, and you cannot become a member of that union until you have passed a comprehensive and rather difficult test on the history of costume.

This test used to be given twice a year, spring and fall, but it is already a crowded field in the sense that there are not enough plays for each member to work as much as he might like, or financially need to. The top people still get most of the good jobs. So the testing has been cut to once a year, and if you fail it the first time, it is possible to repeat, but you will have to wait a year for that second try. The exact rules of this steeplechase—or perhaps obstacle race would be a more appropriate term—are subject to change. So for the last word, get in touch with Local 829 directly. Headquarters were, at the time of this writing, in the Hotel Belvedere, on West Forty-eighth Street. Someone there will give you the name of the current chairman of the Admissions Committee and where he can be reached. The following information, while it is up to date at this moment, should be taken only as an example:

The next test will be given _____ and will be held at the Hotel _____ from nine to four. Be on time, you will need every minute of it. There will be a break for lunch, which will be provided. The fee will be thirty-five dollars, but there is already talk of its being raised to fifty. If you fail, this sum is not refundable. It will cost you an equal amount to repeat it next year—which you may do. There were about thirty people who took it the year I did, and only three became new admissions.

After you have filed for the test, you will be called in to be screened by one or two members of the Admissions Committee. One of the things to be established is whether you are the "right sort." . . . Just what the right sort is I should hesitate to guess, so I can give no hints on how to behave. The union body seems to consist of all sorts, sexes, colors, and even the nationalities vary, which is one of the best things about it. You do not need to be a college graduate, and it is perfectly all right to be a heathen. I would not recommend excessive rudeness, and I don't suppose I would wear a bathing suit for that interview, but it is certainly not necessary to conform to the *beau ideal,* say, of a museum curator.

You will probably be asked to bring along samples of your

work. Take anything you have that is good, sketches, photographs, even advertisements if you have done work in a field that has produced them. If you have designed costumes for a little theatre or a college play, that would be fine, of course. They looked at a fair cross section of my lifework up to that point, mostly sketches and photographs of custom-made dresses, and took a fair amount of time over it, so I suggest a full portfolio, if you can gather it together. There doesn't seem to be any reason why drawings whipped up the night before aren't perfectly legal samples of your work.

Unless you are fortunate enough to be a graduate of the Yale Theatre School, Carnegie Tech, or Pratt Institute, and have one hundred percent recall of everything you learned about the history of costume, the next weeks of your life will now be devoted to studying—hard. It took me a good three months to prepare for that examination, working during the day, studying every night, at mealtime, riding buses or subways. If a friend came over for a drink he was given a glass for one hand, and a series of trial questions from which to cue me in the other. The dining room table was covered with reference books, open or with placemarks, and my family said that every night they expected to find bits of early English armor in the beef and kidney pie, or to be served a fried farthingale instead of frijoles. . . .

The test itself is a very comprehensive one, going back to the earliest presentations of recorded clothing, so don't neglect the Egyptians, Etruscans, and Cretans. It may extend as far up as the 1920s, possibly even the 1930s. Be able to identify the period as to century and half century up through the Middle Ages, break it into quarter century until fifteen hundred, and be prepared to quibble over ten-year differentials the closer you come to your own navy-blue single breasted. Consider not just the suit and dress, the robe and gown, but remember the military gentlemen and their armor. They were a large portion of the population, one way or another, through most of civilization, and it is a good idea to know which came first, chain mail or solid plate, and who wore leather armor. Do you know a baldric from a halberd? When did cartridge cases originate? Do you know a gorget from a greave? Do you know where to find out? There is a pretty good collection of armor at the Metropolitan, and there is also a film on the subject that can be run for you at a special showing if you make proper application. There are also some wonderful books on the subject in the Costume Department of the Metropolitan, ditto at the New York Public Library, main branch, and at the Brooklyn Museum (they are real specialists in the history of clothing).

There are so many good books on the subject that it is hard to single out a few. People will have their own favorites anyway, and the choice depends a great deal on how visual you are in your study preferences. Some feel that the printed word is the definitive authority, others learn best by simply looking at a picture. If you don't know which type you are, this will be a good time to find out. Personally, I found almost everything I wanted in Racinet's *Le Costume Historique,* for as far as it went, but it is hard to get hold of, and very expensive. If you can get it, the complete edition is certainly what you want most for Christmas. Skip the Chrysler convertible, this will take you further. *What People Wore* by Douglas Gorsline is another good one, and much less expen-

sive—mostly a picture book. And Grace Langley-Moore is
one of the great authorities on recent clothing. And fun, too.
She may show you the Civil War period in photographs with
Vivien Leigh wearing a ball gown, and Bea Lillie done to
the nines as a coquette of the Gay Nineties.

The main thing about studying for this examination is to
know where and what to study. The picture books of costumes are not enough. You will need the vocabulary as well.
For example, you may encounter fifty questions on the identification of such words as calash, fascinator, paten, toga,
tunic, wimple, miter, tabard, domino, cowl, redingote, spor-
ran, camisole, peruke, periwig, tippet, rat, fall, and codpiece.

One of the most fascinating, but difficult unless you have
had a classical education, sections of the examination is that
dealing with the identification of famous paintings. A blow-
up of a small portion of an old master—the head of a page
boy from a lower corner of a Murillo, or a square inch of
one of the Breughel *Seasons* that will enlarge to show things
one hadn't dreamed were in the painting. From the haircut
and the shape of the cap you must identify the Florentine,
give his date and period of dress, or place the Breughel peas-
ant in his proper locale and niche in time.

Actually, this is a very sound method of studying. Whenever you have an hour or so drop in at the Metropolitan, or
any museum where you can find even a few of the great old
masters. You will rarely find costume sketches better executed, or more exact. Look at the Vermeer painting of *Lady
at a Casement,* for instance, or *The Christening.* Some of the
best costumes ever executed! And who can explain a Watteau
pleat better than it can be understood by a good long look at

one of Watteau's well-dressed nymphs? Franz Hals, Rembrandt, Gainsborough, Goya, David, Rubens, Giorgione, or those wonderful stiff American Primitives, or Copley, or Stuart . . . or Daumier, or Hogarth—it's mouth-watering just to run through some of the names. Anyway, memorize the dates of the painter, try to register a mental photograph of the paintings in your mind, and if you have total recall you'll have the nicest "pony" that ever went to a quiz on a mental cuff. Also, by the way, you'll have a personal pleasure out of doing your homework that is apt to last much longer than the test itself.

Another one of the questions might run something like "Name at least five sources to which you would refer if you were asked to do costumes for *Camelot* or *Camille*." Costume books, of course—but in the case of *Camelot,* don't forget tapestries and pictures of tombs of early English knights. The idea here is to be inventive, but not too fanciful. Consider, for instance, the usefulness, for certain plays, of such things as travel posters of the different countries; Greek or Roman statues, with especial reference to hairdos; Oriental kakemonos, vases, carvings; antique shows and thrift shops for costumes of the nineteen tens, twenties, thirties; old magazines, newspaper files, photographs, and advertisements; and let's not forget family photograph albums and, sometimes, foreign shops, importers, dealing in the merchandise of the country or period. It's wonderful how much information a storekeeper who is really an authority on his subject can give you if properly approached.

This list is only to start you thinking in all directions. I am sure you are making a better one of your own at the moment.

There is only one way to study for the last half of the test —brush up on your Shakespeare. So far as it is possible to find out, the assignment has always been to design, draw, and render in color finished sketches for the costumes of the principal characters of one of Shakespeare's plays. They are fair enough to assign one of the more famous ones, and sometimes there has been a choice, but aside from that the area cannot be limited any more definitely. Four or five sketches is presumably enough.

There are, roughly, three ways to approach the designs for one of these plays. The first, to do it in modern dress, had better be dismissed as being unsatisfactory to the board of examiners in this particular instance. But you can design them either in the dress of the historical period in which the play takes place—*Macbeth* circa 1050—or in the costume of the years during which Shakespeare wrote the plays and they were produced. Unless you are equipped with the kind of ESP that will give you advance information on which play will be chosen, you are better off to stick to the bard's own time and place.

What else to tell you? Neatness does count. Try and finish —and by now you are probably going to feel pressed for time. Don't get all five done in black and white and not have time to color any of them. Attention will be paid to detail if you use it—the authenticity of shoes and jewels is important. And for heaven's sake bring *all* your own tools, paper, paints, pencils, brushes, a glass for water, a paint rag, pencil sharpener, and, of course, an eraser.

One of the interesting things about this entire examining process is that you will be presumed to be literate. You are supposed to know the story of *Othello,* or *Hamlet,* and who the chief characters are, and what special features in dress the action requires. Is Mercutio a messenger who should have dusty boots? Does Desdemona throw a cloak around her night dress? Is Candide the French for Candida? Or is *Androcles and the Lion* as Greek as it sounds, therefore requiring hyacinthine hair?

Somewhere during this ordeal you will be served lunch. Since the object of this hospitality is to avoid your consulting a dictionary while you wolf your hamburger, do not expect too much. . . .

According to the most recent advice received in this quarter, it will take about a month to six weeks to obtain the results of the test. You will be notified by the Examining Committee.

At this point it is impossible to resist a personal digression. I do not approve of this test. For one thing, not everyone wants to design *costumes* for the theatre. It might be that your talent would be simply for modern clothes, and you would have neither call nor desire to tackle an assignment where you needed to know the proper number of ruffles on Queen Victoria's nightgown. But the more important reason is this—you will never do a period piece without researching it first, at the time you are going to work on it. You are not going to trust your memory on this, and very possibly there will be large gaps in your information for this particular play and its requirements. What the union should want to know about you is: Can you do the research properly when the occasion arises?

What would be much more fair, and more applicable, it

seems to me, would be to give each person to be tested one particular, but different, costume play to design. Give the applicant his assignment, one week in which to do the work, and turn him loose. Loose in the library, the museums, and even among his friends. What if he does get help? Does anyone think the working costume or set designer doesn't get help when on the actual job? It is just as true here as it is all through life, that it isn't what you know, it's who you know. What if someone also has told you that boots of that period laced up the sides, not the front? The art of the designing and the presentation itself are still yours.

After you have taken the test as it stands, see if you approve of this idea. If you do, perhaps you can suggest it to the executive board.

Well, now you are on your own, after the payment of an initiation fee of $7.50. For that sum you will receive a membership card, a dues book, and a copy of the rules. Carry the first in your wallet, keep the second promptly up to date, and study the third. Ignorance of the rules is no excuse.

Some of what you need to know is on the contract, which will be given to you at the union office in sets of three whenever you need them. One is for the producer, one is for the union, and one is for you. Don't do a lick of work on the play until the signed copies are in the hands of Local 829. Read the contract, too, and be sure you know the billing the players will receive. Your rate of pay is affected by that billing.

In the Broadway galaxy there's apt to be confusion among the planets. These tend to get out of orbit and sometimes collide. To know where they belong it is necessary to know a bit about the art of typography. A star is an actor, male or female, whose name appears above the name of the play on the front of the theatre, on the advertising posters, or in the playbill. Sometimes two stars play opposite each other. Sometimes you will have a star and the opposite part is played by the leading man or leading lady, whose name appears next and prominently under the title, usually introduced by "with." A featured player follows. His name appears on the program in large type above the section that is usually termed "cast in order of appearance." The larger the type the more featured the player, but the number of type points scored in this part of the game is of concern only to the actor and his agent.

You will be paid fifty dollars for each costume you design for a star or featured player. The rate for each costume designed for a supporting performer is twenty-five dollars. The rate is still fifty dollars for each costume you find or select, rather than design, for a star or featured performer. But it is only twenty dollars for finding or selecting a supporting player's outfit. The union will be very cross with you for not getting all the money you should, which will happen if you don't know that so-and-so is a featured player.

To give you an idea of what your future standard of living will be like, the following data comes from the most recent contract:

The amount of your fee will be paid you in three parts, on certain specified dates, through the union. The union will retain one percent of whatever you earn, which will be deducted before the moneys are turned over to you.

The money you are given to *spend* for the costumes will be paid out separately through the business manager's office, and is discussed in another chapter.

Let's see how much you may earn if, say, you are designing costumes for a play with one star, two featured players,
and three other characters. The star and featured players
have, respectively, four and three changes each. Of the other
actors, one has two outfits; the other two, one each. This
means ten costumes at fifty dollars each, which equals five
hundred dollars, and for the minor parts at twenty-five dollars each another hundred dollars; so the total fee comes to
six hundred dollars.

Where it says repeats in the contract, this means several
costumes that are identical, in other words, a chorus. If you
have six girls, you will charge one full fee, twenty-five, plus
five "fitting" repeat charges at ten dollars each, or a total of
seventy-five dollars for each female chorus outfit. Ditto for
the male chorus. Of course with the recent trend to individual costuming for each member of the chorus, it is more
likely that you will be in a position to charge a full designing
fee for each one of the "gypsies."

It is a simple, inescapable fact that you cannot design costumes for the Broadway theatre unless you belong to the
union, and that you cannot belong to the union unless you
pass the entrance test. For most ordinary human beings, this
is the biggest obstacle in the race, until you have passed it
and gone on to discover new hazards of your own. Such as,
the problem of finding a job. . . .

3

First—Read the Script!

Let's assume now that you have reached that first desirable plateau where a producer has sent you a script to consider and estimate. What do you do first? Go home, lock all the doors, turn off the radio, refuse to answer your telephone, and read that script carefully. Please read it very carefully, every word of it, including all stage directions and the author's description of the set. There are several reasons for this.

When you were a child, did you ever read a story in which it said that the prince mounted his sable charger and rode to the west, but when you looked at the accompanying illustration the hero was definitely astride a white horse? Or in your more recent maturity haven't you picked up a paperback in which the heroine is lovingly described by the author as having hazel eyes and raven locks, but that dish on the cover is certainly a baby-blue-eyed blonde? And from the intimacy implied in the drawing that girl just has to be the girl who gets him—or else it's the cover for a sequel? You are being considered for a job that involves doing part of the illustrations for a play and the playwright, producer, director, and even the audience—if you were to get that far—all expect you to be thoroughly familiar with the text. If the script says the second woman puts her alligator bag on the couch beside her, the playwright means just that. And you can't change that bag to bright red just because you think that red would be much more interesting with that shocking pink suit she's wearing without going through channels. Chances are you will wind up with the alligator, one hundred and fifty dollars' worth, and there goes your budget if you were counting on getting away with the twenty-five you knew you would pay for a perfectly adequate red bag.

Which brings us to the second reason for reading the script carefully—money. The producer is going to ask for your estimate of what it will cost to costume the play. Then he will scream, cut your figure in half, and the argument will be on. But you will have to have a figure to cut in half and this is how you arrive at it.

Count every character and every outfit he is scheduled to wear. If there is a distinct status differentiation between some of the parts, better divide them in two columns; but if the clothes are all to be custom made, remember it costs just as much to dress the maid as the mistress doing it via Brooks. Go over this list and add accessories: shoes, hose, handkerchiefs, belts, braces, even cuff links if the men are wearing French cuffs, and underwear, if it is special enough to affect the look of the costume worn over it. For example, the crinoline petticoat needed to distend a teen-age party frock is up to the management. Hats of course must be included, and wigs or hair-laces if the part requires a hairdo the actor doesn't grow normally. Occasionally an agreeable actor, usually one of the men, will offer to wear his own tiepin or congress gaiters, but don't count on it ahead of time. Few actors are rich enough to be able to leave any of their personal wardrobe at the theatre for the run of the play. Sometimes an actor in a smaller part, modern dress, will offer to sell the management a suit or a pair of shoes he owns; this is fine if the article is right and will save you money, as you usually pay only about half price.

There is one tricky thing you need to know about the wardrobe of male stars, leading men, and featured players. If the actor is to get over two hundred and eighty dollars a week, he is required to furnish his own clothing, as long as it is modern dress and can be considered part of a normal well-dressed man's habitual wear. This would not apply of course to a dove-gray morning suit nor the bright red smoking jacket we persuaded onto Walter Slezak in *The Gazebo*. Walter didn't think a man his size should wear a red faille jacket and didn't own one. So we had it made for him, paid for it out of the producer's pocket, and proved to an actor how charming it can be, sometimes, to be arrogant about being overweight.

For the rest, rules vary about what is *de rigueur* in the male wardrobe. Last I looked, black tie was in, white tie out, so you'd better check, and the source is Actors' Equity.

The costumer will be paid his usual fee for the supervision of coordinating these male star outfits into the show. You may even have to recommend a change in the color of a necktie but you do not figure these items in the costume estimate proper.

One of the major decisions is into which price range the look and quality of the clothes should fall. Management will tell you that these clothes are simple, nothing to 'em, you can get them at Ohrbach's. I have, but it depends on what you are looking for. If the play is a simple little comedy about well-to-do people, you may need a very expensive wardrobe. Take any Claudette Colbert play. Women drag their husbands to the theatre just to gasp over Miss C. doing the family marketing in a simple little polka-dot outfit that probably cost five times the rent money, and while the insiders protested, I am sure the women from all five boroughs loved it. The clothes can lighten and brighten a comedy. They can get an audience in the gay sophisticated mood that will make them laugh at the fey sophisticated jokes. So fight for enough money if you think the play really needs that kind of costuming. But never do it just to make a bigger job for yourself. Word gets around that you think that way and it will harm your reputation.

The third reason for a careful reading of the script is for a complete understanding of the intellectual content. Just as much as the actor or director—and, I believe, sometimes more than the scene designer—the costumer has to begin the interpretation of the part to the audience. Sometimes it is possible that the clothing can go even further than the playwright has in the writing to reveal the inner identity of the character.

Let us explore this idea some more by example. Say that we have a play in modern dress—then the terminology will be clear to everyone. Say also that the character is a woman because there is more leeway in what you can do with feminine clothes. Don't neglect, however, the possibilities in men's attire. Consider the implications to be drawn from leaving one tab of a button-down shirt sticking up, the choice of a narrow and too short dark tie against a very broad expanse of white shirt when the man should wear a gray shirt and a not too contrasting wider tie with diagonal stripes. Or what would you think of a man foppish enough to wear a smoking jacket and then spill ashes all down the front of it?

But back to our problem lady. Say she is the heroine of a light comedy and the author has simply specified, "Mary is wearing a simple housedress." But what do you as the costume designer who has read the entire play want to say in addition about Mary?

First, that she is a woman—but what kind of woman? Shy? Full-fledged? Childish? Unawakened? The kind who wishes she had been born a boy? Then how old is she— leaving the actress's actual age out of it? Is she rich or poor, fastidious or sloppy? Is she, at the moment the curtain goes up, happy, gay, relaxed, or is she coping with a problem that makes her tense and nervous? Is she artistic, does she have a sense of the appropriate thing to wear? What, aside from her wealth or lack of it, is her status? Is she a nice girl or a provocative tease?

Think about it for a few minutes. You can answer all these questions by your choice of that two-word specification— simple housedress. On top of which, nine times out of ten, you will want to make the actress look pretty. If you can do all this the actress will, whether she knows it or not, be grateful to you. "I don't know why but somehow the damn clothes helped me get off the ground in that sticky first act," was one of the nicest compliments ever.

Now let's dress that heroine. Choose any actress you like, someone whose actual age is between twenty-five and thirty-five. Supposing we dress her according to this formula: The simple housedress is going to be of cotton in a drab color, blue-gray or moss green or that most terrible color of all: tan. It will be cut shirtmaker style with an ugly sleeve length that ends shapelessly just above the elbow. The cut itself is skimpy —not fitted, which would show pride in her femininity—but just a little too tight in some places, too loose in others, the wrong ones. The dress is buttoned all the way up to the throat as this woman is afraid to display any flesh. The cheap plastic buttons are ugly and overlarge, another sign of inadequate taste. The shoes are scuffed brown moccasins, last year's street shoes become this year's house shoes. She wears stockings since no flesh may be revealed, but they are a shade off and too thick. Her hair is set, but stiffly in an unbecoming fashion. The one bright thing about her appearance is a ribbon worn in her hair tied in a bow on top. This is because she is still sexually immature at, say, thirty, and she wishes she were still a late teen-ager, when it was all right never to have been kissed. One or two locks of hair have escaped from the ribbon and keep falling in her face, but instead of retying the bow she occasionally pushes her hair back revealing her tension. Her mouth is made up small and tight and her nail polish is chipped and peeling. The dress itself is of poor quality and shows a lack of both taste and money status. Need we go on?

Now take the same heroine, put her in a simple housedress, but a different one. Again a shirtmaker if you like, but this one is a rose-colored gabardine, marvelously becoming to her hair and skin and, incidentally, attractive in the color scheme of the room. It fits her to perfection—in at the waist, out at the bustline—and is open at the throat just as far as the law allows but not one inch further. Her sleeves are rolled to show a fair amount of healthy skin, her shoes are simple pumps with slender heels, her hose nicely transparent. Her hair is becoming, not chichi, but fashionable enough, and looks well brushed. Her nails are impeccable, her mouth full and generously colored. The dress shows quality in its cut and fabric and a further indication of her background is the good string of short pearls at her neck. Her attention to detail is shown in the matching pearl earrings, button ones. Her imaginative color sense shows in her shoes, which are a glossy dark green, little leaves to the rose of her dress. If she is done right, you should be able to smell her perfume, which is Arpège.

Let's do one more: the provocative tease. This housedress is not a shirtmaker but has a scoop neckline, possibly a little too low, is a print, gay, rebellious, moody or violent, whichever you need to show. Her makeup is sexy and defiant. Legs are bare and her shoes are spike-heeled and more sensual than suitable. Her hair is cut in provocative little tendrils and her earrings are the dangly type . . . do you get the picture?

These are only very broad examples, but they are enough to illustrate the point. The really good working designer will always use some variation of this technique, though the wording may be altogether different. It may be as simple and instinctive as, "That girl wouldn't be seen dead in a dress like that!" or "That man would never own that kind of suit" or "That hat is just exactly right for her." Someone else might say, "That parti-colored dress is completely typical of her ambivalence toward him at this stage of their developing relationship." They can all be talking about the same thing.

A reading of the play with an effort toward real understanding can also help in just getting the job. I was being considered for an emergency situation, to do the clothes for the star only of a play that interested me very much. There had been a temperamental disagreement between the lady and the designer, who was still to handle the rest of the show. The out-of-town opening was only three days away and there just wasn't time to choose the wrong designer again. I sat up half the night to read the play and was scheduled for a breakfast date with Miss Nancy Kelly the next morning. We were to meet at Rumpelmayer's at ten, but when I arrived I was greeted by a distinguished-looking man instead of the actress whom I had expected. He introduced himself as Warren Caro, her future husband by the way, and explained that Nancy would be a little late.

We ordered our eggs Benedict and café au lait and I was wondering as we waited, wondering what to talk to this nice stranger about. Not clothes, surely. He solved that problem. As soon as our coffee was poured and the eggs tasted, Warren turned to me. "Tell me, how much money do you think this woman in the play has to spend on her clothes? Has she an allowance?"

I thought for a moment. "About two hundred a month for herself and her child—an allowance from her father."

I had hesitated, but only for the length of time it took me

to flip back in my mind over the pages of *The Bad Seed* looking for clues. Married to a career naval officer just on his way up. Daughter of a widowed college professor in easy circumstances—probably the apple of his eye. A good manager . . . A few minutes later I saw Nancy coming in and Warren went to the door to meet her and undoubtedly to have a word with her in private. It must have been a good word because she sat down all smiles and graciousness. I not only did that play but all her plays as long as I worked in the theatre. And I made the maternity clothes she wore before Kelly Caro was born and which she was wearing when she received the Sarah Siddons award.

Aside from plumbing the character depths, the simple physical logistics are there for the designer to read with the script. Suppose there is a costume change that occurs during a scene rather than between the acts. How much time will there be? Is it a quick change or is there a long ten- or fifteen-minute scene? Is there time for a complete change or must the actor underdress or overdress? Count the pages between the exit and the reappearance of the actor. A rough rule of thumb allows one minute of playing time for each page of the script. If there are only three and a half pages in which to do a complete change the situation is going to call for some ingenuity, and the sooner the designer starts being inventive the better. Make a note now that the show will require a quick-change room. This is a dressing room constructed in the wings just offstage and must be figured in the production costs. Arriving prepared to do battle on these items gives you a decided advantage that a lame "I hadn't realized . . ." simply does not carry. If the management has taken these

things into account already you can just remain silent. But
not to ask for necessities because you didn't know they were
necessities is a long way from the kind of silence referred to
as golden.

But by and large the best reason for reading the script carefully is just, in the now unfashionable words of Tom Paine,
common sense. The more you know about something, the better equipped you are to fight for it. While it would be wrong
to give the impression that life in the theatre is all à la Merrick, there do occur, shall we say, differences of opinion. You
may need to defend your position and your clothes to anyone
from the director, the producer, the actor to the producer's
wife, who has dropped in at the dress rehearsal on her way
home from a hard day of shopping and objects to that last-
act cocktail dress with the beaded top. A seven-hundred-and-
fifty-dollar objection, but she hates jeweled tops—she always
has. If it just so happens that you can thump the script con-
fidently and come up with a little quote from the author in
which he says, "Lisa enters resplendent in a jewel-embroi-
dered gown," it's nice. You might even go so far as to glare at
her. "Right here it says it. Beads!"

But the ultimate reason for a careful reading is you, yourself. If you are really going to make a serious career of the
theatre—if it is a really fine play—it is obvious that careful
study of it will be rewarding. But you can learn even from a
bad play—what not to do. And on the way up, it is often
necessary to do a few bad plays in order to go on earning. If
you can learn to distinguish what the elements are that make
it a bad play, the time will come when you will be able to
decide between one play and another and choose wisely.

The name of a great star on the marquee may help swell that line at the box office. Talk of a beautiful or elaborate production is an added incentive to the hesitant theatregoer. But neither of these factors can be self-supporting. Without that author with an idea or a thing he wants to say, you have nothing. Producers know it; actors know it. The fabulous invalid would be at death's door indeed without that man that makes with the words, and when we have a poor season on Broadway it is usually because we have poor writing on Broadway. So, begin at the beginning—with the play. It's really the thing.

4

Designing versus Finding

A "found" show is not one you just happen to stumble across in the street, like what we used to call "found money." In fact the term has nothing to do with the means of acquiring the assignment to costume the play. How you get the job is your own business. Maybe you did just stumble over it. If so, better keep the wheres and hows to yourself or you may find a sudden rush of competition to that neighborhood.

No, the expression refers to the method of obtaining the clothes with which to dress the show. Sometimes, usually for monetary reasons, you must shop for the clothes and buy what you can locate in the stores, rather than have the costumes made to your order. Occasionally there is a taste reason involved. In a play such as *Raisin in the Sun,* dealing with a financially pressed Negro family, it would be silly and out of order to have custom-made clothes. The right kind of clothes for these people were chiefly out of Ohrbach's, which is where I "found" them, except for the Nigerian costume, which I made out of a Guatemalan tablecloth and a few safety pins.

The designer gets paid twenty dollars per supporting performer's costume for a found show as opposed to twenty-five dollars for a designed one, and the savings are effective to the production all the way. There is a differentiation in rates all the way down to the walk-ons. Perhaps it sounds like a great deal less work, but don't be fooled. It isn't always so. Sometimes what you are going to be looking for is out of season. Say that the play, scheduled to open mid-December, is a story about people sweltering in July heat. Try to find those seersucker suits, classic embodiment of the sweltering male, in stores preparing to cope with the Christmas holiday!

We had that problem once with Iggie Wolfington, a very funny man whose girth is exceeded only by his sense of comedy. We tried all the outsize emporiums from Barney's to Sixth Avenue, only to be told to come back about mid-July. Finally, because I knew somebody who was the friend of somebody VIP, a major fashion store produced striped seersucker in the necessary size from the warehouse where it stored the classic holdovers from one season to the next. This was a valiant offer and we were perfectly willing to wait the ten days it would require to get this done. But can you see how simple this matter would have been if the budget had allowed me to have had this one suit made?

There is a postscript to this story that has absolutely no bearing on the chapter heading. The script called for this suit to look rumpled, tired, well worn. As soon as it had been fitted to Iggie and delivered to the theatre we began to work on the aging process, having the actor wear it every day to rehearse in, sending it to a laundromat every night. But the fabric was good, or stubborn, cloth. It remained crease resistant and new-looking. Mr. Wolfington began to worry. He started his own series of operations on the costume. He dusted the stage with it. He jumped on it with heavy outdoor shoes. He swears he slept in it and that with it on he rubbed his shoulders against the brick walls of the theatre alley. Finally, it was the most beat-up suit you can imagine. The play opened in New York. The play closed in three days. The producer was one of the generous ones. The actors were allowed to keep their costumes. The producer was also the star of the play. The star had worn a two-thousand-dollar wardrobe. Iggie carried home his forty-dollar cotton suit demolished by his own hand—and feet. And just imagine what a free suit means to an actor suddenly out of work!

Back to business: the main drawback of a found show is that it will violate any preconceived ideas of dress already in the minds of either yourself or the actor. Suppose that scene leaps to life in your eye with the ingenue wearing a red and pink striped shift. There is absolutely no red and pink shift to be found—although six months from now you will see them on every woman in town. This is perfectly natural since it is part of your function to be several months ahead of fashion. Keep your red and pink stripe in mind, and then shop for something that will do the same thing. Perhaps a pink and white print? Finding for a show is often a series of second choices.

Next comes the question of alterations. NO READY-MADE GARMENT EVER FITS WELL ENOUGH TO BE WORN ONSTAGE WITHOUT METICULOUS ALTERATIONS. Things you cannot even see on the street emerge as eyesores behind the footlights. You may have to duplicate the price of the garment in corrections, but it is worth it if they are the right ones. Perfect fitting can remove the price tag from a cheap dress.

Whenever it is possible, if the store has a *good* alteration department, make them responsible for the corrections. If they are getting program acknowledgments they will do their best to make the finished product look as attractive as possible, and they have access to resources beyond you, such as getting material with which to face a hem or getting a new belt direct from the manufacturer. Otherwise, you will have to find your own alteration hand, and if you ever do locate a top-notch one, marry her yourself if you're a man, even if it makes you a bigamist, or, if you're of the same sex, either marry her to your brother or your favorite cousin. Your wardrobe woman may tell you she can sew, yes, she can do all those things. Don't believe her. If she were first-rate, she would have a year-round job with benefits at a fine store, instead of living among the hazardous peaks and troughs of Broadway. If necessary, try her out on an alteration on something of your own. It may cost you a bit but it will be a worthwhile investment.

On the other hand, there are distinct advantages to a found show. Both you and your actor can see how the garment looks, on, in the flesh, before you are committed to it. Any emotional antireactions can be uncovered ahead of time. And, if you have a large enough try-on room, you can preview that second-act cocktail party in full dress, and see how the various costumes react on each other. What might look like a balanced dinner party on paper might swing in favor of the tall nonentity in royal blue. . . .

The advantages of the designed show spring to mind at once. You can have what you want, what you feel is right. You can really fit the clothes, not only to the actors but also to your script. And it can be June in January, for all you care.

The designed show is certainly the quickest way to fame and possibly fortune. You can get private customers from it if you have your own atelier. At its best, you are giving a fashion show every night with good lighting on the best models in the world, to a captive and affluent audience of clothes-conscious women and the men who pay their bills. You can be as creative as you please. You can state in cloth your own ideology about style. At the worst, if nobody likes the clothes, you must take all the blame on your own bowed and aching shoulders. You did it, all by yourself.

There are things to be said on both sides of this fence. It is easier, in case you are that popular, to do several found shows at one time. You can overlap your shopping as well as your shows. On the other hand you can fit the script and your actresses better via the workrooms of Brooks Costume and your own sketches.

One interjection. I have never heard of either a costume play or a musical being found shows, except off-Broadway, and even then it is hard.

There is no sense in arguing any more of these pros and cons ahead of time. The ones mentioned are only to give you examples. You will develop your own preferences as you become experienced. The type of production and the size of the budget are established factors long before the costume designer is engaged, and it is only in rare instances that he can dictate. The thing to do is to consider the advantages to whichever kind of play you are doing, and go ahead, accentuating the positive.

There are some theatrical designers who would rather create their own clothes than eat. If you are one of these the findings play will be frustrating. On the other hand, there is the artist who can be appreciative of and make excellent use of the originations of other people, sometimes adding of course a little fillip of his own. To say that there are no fine ready-to-wear clothes in America would be silly. Just because one is an author, one cannot claim that there are no other writers worth reading. There are still Joyce, Kafka, Dostoevski, to be admired. This is true in all the arts, and designing for the theatre is, I believe, one of the arts.

Ingenuity is one of the prerequisites of the designer of the found show. On one occasion I stepped in to redo the wardrobe of a star who refused to appear in the clothes that had been presented to her by a designer she felt didn't know his business. It was three days before the out-of-town tryout and there was no time to have the clothes made. So rehearsal was called off for just one afternoon, which was all the time that could be spared that late in the game. Fortified by lunch at the Plaza, we sallied forth to do battle at my favorite specialty shop, where I had already spent the morning lining up possibilities.

There were five outfits required. Everything went swimmingly from the beginning. The first-act pink was just right, ditto the negligee. The third change was all right, and the fourth was even more becoming than I had hoped. Even number five was fine, except for one thing: it had to have sleeves. Wisely, the actress knew that she looked better with the tops of her arms covered. But—the manufacturer was a Californian. We called Los Angeles. No, the dress could not be reordered with sleeves. There just wasn't any more material at the factory. We sat in the dressing room and listened to each other's hearts breaking and stared at the so almost-perfect dress hanging there . . . two almost perfect dresses in fact, because we had found the actress needed a smaller size than the one she had first tried on.

It was simple. I called back the departing fitter and asked if she could make sleeves. Of course she could—out of the back of the skirt of the second dress. And the dress, though just right, was inexpensive, even cheap. Forty-five dollars. We were allowed three or four times that on our emergency budget. So for ninety dollars, a small alteration charge, and a little headwork, we had a dress so successful that when the play became a movie, the Hollywood studio reproduced it, line for line, at about twenty times its original cost.

That second dress with two holes the exact shape of short sleeves cut in the back of the very full skirt bothered me for weeks. It was exactly the size of my teen-age daughter. And a color she loved. So one night I took the dress apart, cut a slimmer skirt with no holes, and put it back together again. It fit Amanda like the proverbial glove. So you see—first ingenuity, then serendipity. I abhor waste.

5

How to Begin...
at the Beginning

Unless special arrangements have been made you may not meet any of the cast until the first day of rehearsal. Actors' Equity has strict rules regarding the time to be spent on costuming to avoid overworking the actors. By and large this is a good thing and it may provide you, while you are getting your feet wet, with some sort of standard by which to measure your own efficiency.

Most plays, barring an out-of-season tempest or hurricane, can be costumed in the time allowed by Equity. The solution is often to bring things to the theatre rather than to have the performer chase around with you.

First day of rehearsal usually means a reading with everyone, director, stage manager, and yourself included, sitting on stage around a large table. This will at least give you a chance to observe the faces and try to fasten the names that go with them firmly in the right places. This is important. To the actor, no matter how small a part he may be playing at the moment, the recognition of his name is one of his standards of achievement. Not to recognize or to forget his name is an ego body blow that is not the designer's business to deliver.

The one thing you will want this first day is a complete set of measurements—of the entire cast. Ask the stage manager to lend you a dressing room for this purpose and as you see the opportunity lure your victims off to submit to the tape measure in privacy. Never ask anyone to be measured in front of the rest of the company. Never believe an actress who tells you anything relative to the size of her waist, hips, or feet. And Nancy Kelly and Vicki Cummings are almost the only actresses who *really* wear size four and a half shoes.

That tape measure should be in your pocket for your first reading with the actors as well as a working pencil and a small notebook. Carry that notebook with the measurements and size information duly recorded until the day after the Broadway opening, at least—it is your bible for this production. In case of fire, save it first, yourself afterward. You will never realize how valuable it is until some moment when you find yourself without it.

Get *all* the measurements and sizes, even ones you think you will not need. For one thing this thoroughness flatters the actor—it sounds as if you are giving great attention to every detail of his wardrobe. Again, you can never tell when some revision in the script is going to call for a cowboy hat for the butler and you cannot reach the man who is playing the butler to ask him for his head size because he lives in Far Rockaway and has an unlisted phone.

That's another thing; get everybody's phone number. Either remember to ask the actors or get them from the stage manager later. Working on a play without this list of often unlisted numbers would be comparable to trying to hold down a job as nurse at a kindergarten without a supply of adhesive plasters.

You will need:

FOR THE WOMEN

Dress size, waist, bust, and hip measure.

Size of bra, slip, briefs.

Shoe, stocking (regular, tall, or short), gloves, head size.

Does she wear a different blouse size from her dress?

And, perhaps, wedding ring measure!

FOR THE MEN

Get *complete* specifications, such as "46, tall, portly, 34-inch inseam."

Belt size.

Shirt-, neck-, sleeve-length plus any collar particulars, shoe, sock, glove, hat size.

Sometimes size of pajamas.

Of course if the costumes are to be custom made the exact measurements will be taken by the expert wherever the clothes are being executed. Do not take these measures yourself and provide them for the dressmaker or tailor . . . make the dressmaker or tailor take their own measurements. No two people take measures alike and in this way the blame may fall on you if the finished garment doesn't fit.

If you can afford the time, go to the first rehearsal when the actors are on their feet moving around. Don't watch this from the wings. Sit down in the orchestra or station yourself behind the last row of seats, depending on your eyesight. What you are looking for now is to see how these people move around. They will probably not have started to "characterize" yet and what you will be watching will be their natural movements. Is there a slight tendency to favor one foot or a stiffness of joints? Is there a certain austerity or angularity or does that fifty-year-old character woman move with the unexpected grace of a young dancer? Does so-and-so trip over his own feet? Perhaps he has never been shod correctly. This can be as true of a human being as a horse.

At any rate this is all knowledge the good designer should have, even though sometimes there is nothing he can do about it. But there is a good deal that can be done if you know the tools of your craft. Perhaps that angular ingenue should never wear those straight, tight little dresses. Certain fabrics, jersey for instance, used generously and with enough fullness, can simulate fluidity and grace. Or perhaps the author wants that acrobatic and extroverted young lead to appear constrained and inhibited in the opening. So swaddling clothes are indicated for that baby to begin with. Is the heroine just a little too tall for the hero? That is going to mean a lowered heel for her and perhaps Adler Elevators for him.

If this is to be a "designed" show, now is the time to turn those rough working sketches into finished drawings. Before any of them are put in work remember that every accepted sketch is supposed to be initialed by the producer. In case of arguments he *can* refuse to pay for anything not initialed.

It is a good idea to get estimates from several of the costume companies on the cost of execution. Here there is a wide choice and it can range through Brooks, Eaves, Manhattan, to any rare discovery of your own, though you must use only a costume manufacturer with a union workroom. Personally, for any traditional costume play I have a weakness for Brooks. We have had our fallings-out during moments of stress, but in the long run they have always somehow gotten the clothes there on time—even by special messenger to Philadelphia once—and they do know their business. One of the great dangers with new people is that they may produce something that looks as unprofessional as if mother had whipped it up for the senior play at school. This, decidedly, is not a Brooks failing. Odysseus will emerge godlike from their hands. But with modern dress, you can be perfectly safe with some small workroom (still union, though) of your own discovery.

Work cannot commence until all the actors have been up to be measured by the executing company itself and until you have okayed the fabric swatches for quality and exact color. You may want to give a hand on shopping for these—nobody will mind if you take on this chore.

There is another way in which modern dress clothes are custom made these days and that is when one of the big designers from Seventh Avenue does them. Pauline Trigère, Scaasi, and some others have been notably successful with their designing for the theatre, having as they do a real sense of the drama in clothing. Whether you can arrange this depends on your connections, your female star, and your budget. Here is no money-saving gambit. It is not like "I can get it for you wholesale." Time will be a factor, too. The best time to ask is not just exactly when a new line is about to open. But you, the management, and the manufacturer can all appreciate the publicity value of "Clothes by Trigère."

For the men's clothes, modern, custom made, one of the happiest and most successful connections I have ever lucked onto is Davidoff, on lower Broadway. Dave Daynard, the owner and the company's best public relations man, must have dressed about every male star in the business by now and has kept many of them as private customers and friends thereafter. This is one of those places where, happily, "the price is right."

What if this is going to be a "found" show? "Findings" is the technical term used for the accouterments of a play that are *bought* ready-to-wear. Better use the variation, "off the peg," while the current rage for English actors continues. Anyway, here we switch from Brooks Costume to Brooks Brothers, who are not even cousins twenty-five blocks removed.

Note: There *is* a relation, however, between Brooks Costume and Brooks Uniform, although you shop at the latter independently. And in case you are waiting to become a member of Local 829 and are meanwhile looking for temporary employment elsewhere, the uniform branch of the family has an excellent stock of outfits for chauffeurs, valets, cooks, maids, chefs, gentlemen's gentlemen, stewardesses, firemen, policemen, and, probably, policewomen.

By now, if you have read the script as thoroughly as was recommended in Chapter 3, you must have an idea of which store or stores are most suitable for the play. Obviously you are not going to dress *Raisin in the Sun* from Bergdorf's no matter how large your budget. Ohrbach's was, and is, just right for that play. But for *Tunnel of Love* Bonwit Teller for the women and Brooks for the men fit nicely in both price and style categories. Or you could do both at Saks Fifth Avenue, which has an excellent and diversified men's department as well as being adept with women. Generally speaking, it is a good idea to put as many eggs as you can in one basket in this business, since the more money you are spending with a store the more likely they are to forgive certain theatrical eccentricities in the way of returns and exchanges. If, however, you have one character who really requires special fitting because of size problems, take him or her to Barney's or Lane Bryant without wasting time or hurting feelings by trying to make a size forty-eight conform to size sixteen measurements. Trying to make an actor fit into the department store's basket of regular sizes—with unsuccessful alterations all over the place—will have him feeling like a square peg before you are through.

Whichever store you select try to shop with each actor individually, not in the confusion of a group. Treat him during this spree as if outfitting him attractively and suitably were the only problem on your mind. Take as much time as you can: be patient. The actor ego is a very live, tangible, and easily damaged commodity and usually gives its best performance when confident and sure of itself. A destructive costume session can easily have repercussive effects in the actual performances.

When I say shop individually I mean begin at the top of course with the star or lead. You cannot award peacock blue as a dress color for that cocktail party scene to the walk-on understudy until you are sure the leading lady is satisfied with her choice of pinkish mauve. I fell into this trap once and was several months working my way out, some of the time on my hands and knees. . . .

It happened in a play in which the second woman was almost of the same stature as the star. Both were excellent actresses, one was a stunning brunette, the other a handsome blonde. Let us say there was rivalry, if not declared friction. I had tried to persuade the star into a vivid red outfit for her second change, the scene in which she and the other woman meet face to face for the first time onstage; but she rejected the idea as too obvious and decided on an elegant and figure-flattering navy blue. So when the other actress fell in love with a knockout red suit that got the approval of author, director, and producer, she was allowed to have it of course. She may have been so pleased with it because when she modeled it onstage there had been a few wolf calls.

There must have been a story conference that night from which I was excluded because the next morning the star told me that Act One had a new scene in which she would have a costume change.

"Good grief!" I exclaimed. "And where are you going to get that at this late date? Can you shop with me tonight after rehearsal?"

She smiled sweetly. "Not necessary, darling. I knew you

were just frantically busy getting shoes and bags for *her* red
suit because it took *her* so long to make up *her* alleged mind
—and I didn't want to bother you with silly me. So I just
took a cab this morning before rehearsal and I've ordered a
simple little sheath from Madame X. She thinks she can have
it in time for me."

"What's it like?" I asked, trying to be casual, but there
were clouds forming in my mind.

"Wait till you see it. It's a surprise." And she floated away.

Mm-hmm. You've guessed it. It was bright red, and stunning. And the star wore it in the scene just *before* that second
woman made her first appearance on stage. For some obscure
reason both of them blamed *me!*

But back to more neutral colors. Whenever possible abide
by an actor's color preferences or dislikes. If it doesn't clash
with the set, conflict with another character, or misinterpret
the part, let the ingenue wear blue, which she loves—don't
put her into the pink she hates. Just as long as there's no reason not to, naturally. He or she will be happier and you may
be able to ask a favor in return, like could so-and-so possibly
wear her own shoes in a pinch and keep quiet about it until
the ones on order arrive from the dyers?

But listen to the way you are told about this predilection.
Was it "—wear any suit as long as it's not brown. I hate
brown suits!"? Or was it "—can't wear brown suits. Never
could. Terribly unbecoming—"? It's just possible you may be
able to prove that a brown suit isn't unbecoming at all, with
a certain change in the makeup base, which is a good idea
anyhow as it makes him look younger and healthier. Very often part of your job will be to destroy an ancient *idée fixe*

that isn't true at all. When you do this successfully, most actors are grateful. If not, they don't need you; they need their
analyst.

Let's take time here for another digression, this one on
Where to Find It. If you have lived for any length of time in
the community in which you are functioning, you have
probably already started to compile a list of resources. Hang
on to it and keep adding to it. This list is one of the designer's
most valuable assets.

I can only speak for New York, which is where I have
worked, but for what it is worth here is a list, haphazard and
varied, of some of my favorite places. If you are in Pittsburgh
or San Francisco the following may be of little use to you and
you may skip this section. Go curl up with a good book. But
if you are in New York, the book may very well be that guide-
to-shopping masterpiece, Kate Simon's *New York Places and
Pleasures*. It tells you where to find everything, from genuine
Indian bleeding madras to a Chinese bed jacket. Whatever
else you buy while you are rushing around unearthing your
costume rarities—such as comestibles or real stone jewelry
(and she lists these too)—will be on your head. Do not send
the bill to me.

A Few of the Best Places in Town for

(*Retail* marked with *R; Wholesale* with *W;* on wholesale
items try phoning first.)

Originala: The most beautiful coats made. *W*

Monte Sano & Pruzan: The other most beautiful coats
made. Different. *W*

Ben Zuckerman: Very handsome clothes. Coats. Suits. Dresses. *W*

Ben Reig: Ditto, only dressier. *W*

Talmack: Dresses. Classically good-looking. *W*

Junior Sophisticates: Just that and good at it. *W*

Trigère: For my money, the greatest American designer— even if she is French. *W*

Coblentz: The place for fine bags if you don't go to Koret. *W*

Koret: The place for fine bags if you don't go to Coblentz. *W*

Milton C. Herman: Furs. For sale or for hire. And Milton is a sucker for the theatre. Will practically give you a mink for opening night tickets. *W*

JEWELRY

Brania: Bryan Bishop says his business is just beads—these are imaginative and irresistible. He will also make you a bead curtain. *W*

Trifari: The ultimate in set stone jewels. Look like real and cost almost ditto. *W*

Delta: Pearls, pearls, pearls. *W*

SHOES

Adler Elevators: Shoes with built-in devices that will make actors tower over their womenfolk. Cowboy boots will help do this too, of course. *R*

La Ray Boot Shop: Stock all kinds of ballet slippers. But they also make shoes to order from Three Musketeer boots to Ben Hur sandals. Not cheap, but they *fit*. *W* and *R*

AND OTHER THINGS

Uncle Sam: Umbrellas. Will make up any kind he doesn't have in stock, which is not many kinds. Need one with a foil in the shaft? Canes too. *R*

Davidoff: Men's clothes. Modern and period. Rave as before. *R*

Anne Benjamin: If you don't know this Third Avenue antique shop already you have a treat in store for you. Best collection in town of authentic clothes going back to the Civil War. Charming and unusual ideas for opening-night gifts too —and buy yourself Christmas presents while you are there. *R*

Gunn and Latchford: Largest supply and color range of Oriental silks. *W* and *R*

Far Eastern Fabrics: Just what it says, in depth. Some Oriental costumes and trinkets, modern school. *W* and *R*

Ohrbach's: Fashion clothes at a price, as well as the expected bargains. The boutique is marvelous, in small sizes. On the executive floor ask for a PR genius named Mark Klausen who is the go-between for the store and the drama. Until you are on his list you will never know how pleasant it is to shop here. He fixes it so you can take things to the theatre, try on there, return the rejects. *R*

Imperial Fabrics, Hester Street: Ask for Lou. The most complete and mouth-watering stock of fashion fabrics from full bolts to remnants. *W*

Hudson Army & Navy: Excellent work clothes. Practically everything a man would wear out of doors. Dungarees, odd-type shirts. *R*

Saks Fifth Avenue, Bonwit's, and *Bergdorf's:* All go without saying. But don't overlook Bergdorf sportswear where you can have the Goodman styling at a price you wouldn't believe. Miss Bergdorf is clever, too. Saks has everything under one roof, men, women, and children. What more can you ask, particularly when it's raining? *R*

Bonwit's: Go to the sixth floor, ask for Miss Traube, and tell her I sent you. Bea is a revelation, in energy, helpfulness, and she is thoroughly stage struck. She and her staff will bring the whole store to your weary feet, produce shoes that match dresses, and perform miracles of special ordering. Best to have a healthy budget but there is no better place to spend it. She can, and does, help you balance it by finding you the forty dollar steal that looks like a million. The reason no other store in town has a department like this is that there is no other woman like her. Don't go there if you object to sharing a dressing room with Joan Crawford or Pegeen Fitzgerald. *R*

THREE FAR-FLUNG RECOMMENDATIONS

Have you a show to do in Dallas? Don't try to avoid the inevitable: go to Neiman Marcus. It is even greater than Texans say; it is as great as Arizona citizens think Goldwater's is. *R*

Opening a play in South Africa? The Shelley Shops, all around and near Johannesburg. See if you can get Vicki Press to come and help you. She is the wife of the owner and the youngest woman I know with her sense of fashion and impeccable taste. *R*

Trying a play out on the Coast? Or got your first crack at a movie and feeling babes-in-the-woodsish? In Los Angeles, go to Western Costume and put yourself at the mercy of Al Nickel. (*R* and *W*) He is one of the three nicest men in town and even if Western doesn't do the show, he will probably help you enough so that you can.

Well, back to work. The first thing is to get every major garment, dress, suit, or robe on order for each member of the cast. When these are in the process of creation or alteration, you can begin filling in the accessories, shoes, bags, gloves, tiepins—and that item I always forgot—belts or suspenders for the men. But keep in touch with rehearsals. It is possible to walk in any day and to find that a whole scene has been put in or taken out. The stage manager, the actress in question, and the director will tell you individually and at length that the handbag that the actress carries on in the second-act opening simply must have a handle to go over her arm, otherwise she won't have enough hands to manage it. You will already have selected one with a handle, having figured that out for yourself, but listen politely. No one will think to tell you that the last scene has now been rewritten so that it is raining when the dark stranger appears out of the night and he will require a raincoat and an umbrella. This is the kind of thing you will have to find out for yourself.

One of the most important people in a costumer's life is the wardrobe woman. Some are absolute jewels; some are not worth the powder to blow up a feather. Until you know good ones and can ask for your favorites by name, you will have to trust the producer or take what the union sends you. Find out if she has her own sewing machine, steam iron, and ironing board and plans to carry them with her out of town. If not, it's dollars to doughnuts she isn't going to carry her share of the show load.

Get her on the show as soon as the producer is willing to begin paying her salary. If you have her early and she is a good seamstress, she can do some of the alterations if the clothes have come, for instance, from Ohrbach's. And you can always put her to work making those muslin sheets for covering the clothes that you will need for every dressing room in the theatre. Let her start collecting hangers, too. There are never enough even with the ones you will both steal from the hotel in New Haven.

You will of course have to have her for the packing out. This is part of her official duty and is usually done from the theatre two or three days before the entire company's official exit for the out-of-town tryout. Sometime before this the company or the business manager will have asked you how many trunks you will need. If you don't know, get the wardrobe woman's opinion, she is usually pretty accurate about this and can estimate from your own list of the clothes. You will also need shoe and makeup boxes, as they are called, since the actors bring their makeup to the theatre to be shipped out at company expense. You may also need hat and/or wig boxes.

The wardrobe will leave by truck, probably along with the scenery, for Boston, Hartford, Bridgeport, New Haven, Wilmington, or Philadelphia. The departure date is scheduled so that the shipment arrives in the tryout town in time for the scenery to be assembled. This is supposed to take two or three days before the company gets there for dress and prop rehearsals—and when the company gets there it will, naturally, not be done. It may not even be unloaded yet. This helps create a feeling of urgency that is highly dramatic.

Except in unusual cases you will not have seen the clothes, finished, on the actors. You will not have seen them with all their accessories and you will not have seen the actors on stage with each other wearing your clothes. You will probably not have seen the set or the furniture assembled on the stage. Well, now you will. Much of it will come as a surprise to you. Let us hope it is a happy one. Part of your insurance policy will come from two other factors. You don't really need to leave everything to chance.

6

The Two Other Designers

Although there may be many times when to the costume designer it will seem that he is going it absolutely alone, actually this will not have been true. There are two other people whose work he must consider in relation to his own. The first of these is the set designer, who takes precedence both in time and rank. He is usually hired well in advance of the costumer simply because it takes longer to build scenery than to build clothes. And he ranks the wardrobe designer in the union, standing as a sort of father figure. Remember that when the scene designer passed his test to get into Local 829 he not only took, and passed, the test for the architectural and artistic work he had done—but he also had to pass the same test the costumer did, and so is qualified to do both sets and costumes, if he so desires.

Luckily for us, few of the scene designers elect to do the costuming. When they do, it is apt to be because of a fondness for a certain period or some other personal predilection.

But even if the designer leaves the costumes strictly up to you, it is well to remember that he could do them if he had the time and the inclination and that he might, under certain circumstances, prove a useful ally. There are specific things you can talk over with him, technical problems that perhaps would not be understood by anyone else in the company. By this I do not mean to let him do your work or to have your ideas for you. If the scene designer had wanted to do your job he would also be getting paid for it.

Like the producer, you too must begin with the set. First, ask to see the sketch and photograph it on your mind as accurately as possible. Then, the grouping of the furniture is important to you because it tells you fairly accurately the immediate background for certain clothes in certain scenes. "Heroine retreats toward rear . . ." Remember that early warning to read your script first?

The next thing you want from the set designer is a complete set of color swatches. Everything. Wall color, draperies, couch and chair upholstery, lampshades, any dominating pictures, even the rug. Remember, the half the house that sits in the balcony and mezzanine will view the actors against a background of floor covering. You will even want to know about vases of flowers and sofa cushions if they are to be at all sizable. And what if your heroine has to carry on that vase of flowers in her magenta tea gown?

You may have to hound your confrere for this information since for some reason swatches are invariably in short supply. But do it—mercilessly. You cannot make a color move until you have this already determined knowledge. It would be like trying to paint a picture without knowing what the background was going to be.

On this same subject equip yourself with samples of everything in your field that is swatchable. Dress, suit, bags, coats, and even a running memo to yourself of the color of a tie or shirt. Take my word for it. You may have to have gloves or shoes dyed to match something and it is so comforting to have the exact sample right there at your fingertips.

If the set designer says, "Wouldn't it be stunning if Lady Agatha wore a yellow something or other in that scene where she sits on the window seat?"—consider it. He just may have a sense of color and fitness equal to your own. And the two of you, though your jobs may be separate and individual, are still painting one picture on one canvas inside that proscenium, not two paintings laid on top of one another and diverging at the edges. But you need not be subservient. If you are against it and for a good reason—explain why. He may have a good visual color sense while your own objection may be for a psychological color reason. It is possible that in a case of this sort you may be sounder and closer to the bone of the character than he is.

The third member of this triumvirate of designers comes into the picture late, after most of the costumer's work is done: this is the lighting expert. What he does for the play can have a very important effect on clothing as far as color is concerned.

The reason his is such a late entry is that there is very little he can do before the set is in place and ready to be lit. This happens at the first out-of-town tryouts, since the completed set goes right from the scenic studio that built it to the theatre at New Haven, Hartford, or even Toronto, on the same shipment that is likely to include the wardrobe trunks. Even an indication of the lighting in advance of the standing sets being in position is almost impossible, for the director is not likely to be through with his work before opening time and the lighting in addition to displaying the scenery has to follow the action around the stage. Though the audience may never realize it, the actors are not performing just in back of a glow of stationary footlights, but with traveling spots that pick them up and accentuate them as clearly or as subtly as the director wishes. And if the director makes a change in the crossing of one character at the last minute, it may necessitate a rearrangement of the lighting chart.

Some scene designers do their own lighting, but not too many of them. A large outfit such as Jo Mielziner's may have its own lighting expert as part of the office, but this is not common. Chances are that the first time you will even get a hint of how your costumes will really look will be long after you can do a blessed thing about it.

If you doubt what I say about the efficacy of light and you are a New Yorker, remember back to the early days of Radio City Music Hall. That cloth of gold curtain was one of the wonders of this temple of pleasure and was supposed to be the most expensive theatre curtain contracted for at the time. If you came into the theatre while the houselights were up it was perfectly plain that the dazzling two thousand yards of fabric in front of you was gold, gold lamé. But while the stage show was in progress that curtain changed more rapidly than a chameleon. It became red, or green or blue or any color Vincent Minelli wanted. Many people thought it was a different curtain, so solid, so through and through did the color seem. Only when the color changed and the curtain had not moved was it clear that it had all been done at the lighting switchboard.

This is an exaggerated example of what lights can do to your clothing, but it is not too far out. The question becomes what can you do to protect yourself? How can you keep that dress that has to be pink from turning pale plum color or a green blue from going off into the sky? If only you had known!

There are a few things you can know, such as the basic lighting colors for a basic kind of play. Most comedies will be lit with pinks and ambers, a mystery play will probably have a preponderance of blue and green for that spooky effect, etc. And either the director or the set designer can tell you way ahead of time what will be the general lighting range. This much is inherent in the script and the director's and scenic artist's interpretation of it.

Since it is obviously impossible to taxi from department store to couturier's salon with an electronic switchboard and a full battery of lights, what can be done to avoid the pitfalls exemplified by that trough that contains the foots? For what it is worth here are my suggestions.

Go to a good theatrical lighting company, such as Knicker-bocker in New York, and get yourself two baby spots. The portable kind I used took up the space of a cube approximately a foot in each direction. At the same place I bought a set of gelatins to fit. These are not diet-conscious desserts or fingernail additives; they are transparent colored squares that slide into the slots of the spotlights and color the light projected by the white globe that lights the fixture. This purchase was not very expensive and worth every one of the few dollars I paid.

Then, when you want to start work on a production, ask the set designer to make a rough estimate of the basic lighting. His answer might be something like this, "Pinks and ambers for the first act, modified to some blue and a little green for Act Two—and then back to pinks and ambers. Strong light at the finish."

With this information you can find out a great deal. Take home samples of your purchased trophies—the belt of a dress, one of a pair of colored shoes, a swatch of the fabric you intend to use for an evening wrap, the hem cut off when another dress was shortened. If you can acquire any of these bits and pieces before you are committed to the purchase, so much the better. Put a pink gelatin in one spot, an amber in another, etc., and see for yourself the effect of the probable lighting in which the play will be viewed by future audiences.

Different textures and surfaces that appear to match in ordinary daylight may respond very strangely under lights, sometimes showing a wide divergence. Some surfaces tend to absorb light, others to repel it. This variance is something you can only tell about by trying it out, so it is a big help to have your own home-sized Bureau of Tests and Standards. Later, if someone points an accusing finger at you when the garment you had announced as being a light red turns up on stage as more of an orange, you can say, "It's that cotton-picking light!" And because you should know what a cotton-picking light is: in the more scientific warehouses where cotton is graded or sorted with reference to length of staple and color, the sorters work under blue lights, usually fluorescent. Blue is used because this color brings out the yellow in the cotton fibers so that the pickers have an easier time distinguishing color quality.

There's an episode involving both the lighting and the costume designers, but the man I feel sorry for is the poor actor. This incident did not happen to me but to the friend of a friend. I see no reason to doubt its genuineness, however, since it would have been hard to invent—while in the theatre if you are just around in it long enough something of the sort is bound to happen.

This raconteur two-times-removed had once played in a theatre-in-the-round production of *Finian's Rainbow*. In case you haven't seen this play, two of the characters are a leprechaun who can perform magic and a Southern senator who hates the Negro race. The exasperated leprechaun finally decides to transform the senator, as a punishment for his way of thinking, into a Negro. All very well in the script but a little harder to do than to read about—and for theatre-in-the-round even more difficult, since almost all activity is carried on in front of an audience. However, they planned to work it this way: the playing area of the theatre had been elevated by a dais. From the dais five ramps led down on which the actors made their entrances and exits. As the magic-maker was to begin his abracadabra there would be a complete blackout, followed by an explosive, multicolored flare—providing just twenty seconds before the lights went up again and revealed the transformed character actor. If not fast, no good—effect lost, naturally.

To make it in time it was planned that the senator would rush down a certain ramp at the moment of darkness where he would be greeted by three attendants completely covered in black. This is an old Japanese device used in that country's puppet theatre, where the manipulators of the Bunraki puppets appear right on stage, black-clothed from head to toe. After a few minutes they so fade from the eyes of the audience as to seem invisible.

Well, as the senator rushed to the end of the ramp he would be seized by his three invisible dressers. The first would strip him of his white Southern politico's suit and the second, kneeling at his feet, would begin zipping him into a trick one-piece black Uncle Tom garb, while the third would apply blackface as rapidly as possible to his cheeks. This was rehearsed and rehearsed until it was timed, on the stage manager's stopwatch, as not one second over twenty—and everyone was confident that the hocus-pocus would work.

Came opening night. The musical revolved as per schedule until the moment of the blackout. Then the actor, nervous and tense because of the split-second timing, ran down the wrong ramp. Naturally he was met on his descent by a nothingness that must have seemed abysmal—no dressers, no black suit, no blackface!

But nothing is ever wasted. There was in the front row of seats a reluctant theatregoer who had been dragged there by his wife, a seeker after culture. This man hadn't wanted to come in the first place, he hadn't liked the musical from the overture—and at this stage of development he was fed up. When the explosion and flare occurred he had had all he was going to take. Deciding to sneak out while the houselights were down, he leaned toward his spouse, hissed, "That does it, Louisa!"—and broke for freedom. He made it just to the end point of that ramp, where he was seized by those three attendants, worried to death because the actor was several seconds late on his exit, and while one helped the reluctant theatregoer to undress, the number-three boy began his generous application of blackface. . . . Wonder if Louisa ever got that man inside a theatre again?

If I were for any reason one could think of to go back and do it all over again—or if I were as young as some of my readers can be presumed to be—I would certainly add a course in stage lighting to my vocational training. It would be the best additional ammunition I can think of, both for getting work to begin with and as a means of broadening one's eventual horizons. Consider it from the viewpoint of the set designer. Isn't it better if he can hire one person to fill in that space on the stage rather than two? From your own view, it is one of the few ways of adding to your fees per production since you can collect both salaries with very little added time being demanded of you. This time usually finds the costumer at the theatre anyway, eyes glued to what is going on as the lighting expert barks out orders to that unseen man up on the grid. And finally, look at how you can benefit yourself, play into your own hands so to speak, by the knowledge of what you are going to do to the costumes created by your alter ego—and why you are going to do it.

7

The Costume Designer
as a Member of the Company

Technically, the costume designer is a member of management. By "management" is meant the producer, company manager, business manager—all those people who are, in a sense, office help. The other side of the coin is the company, by which I mean those members of Actors' Equity who are creating the specific parts on the stage, and their understudies.

Theoretically, there should be no division between these two. Both have the same object, to bring in a successful play that will operate at a profit and bring esteem to all parties concerned. But there are often times, due to temperament, circumstances, and the particular exigencies of some situations, when there may be a split between company and management. If this occurs, the designer is apt to identify himself with the actors for whom he is creating wardrobes.

There are many reasons why this is only natural. The first

is that most of the designer's working time is spent with those actors. The second is that the actors tend to project him onto their side. Just as no man is a hero to his valet, so he has few secrets from him. Under the circumstances of getting a play ready for Broadway, it is normal to make the designer the actor's confidant. Perhaps the schism between company and management has been created by money. I don't mean salaries—these are certainly none of the costumer's business. What I have in mind is the amount to be spent on wardrobe. The second woman is not happy with the twenty-dollar bag selected for her. Out of the corner of her eye she just caught sight of one at seventy-five that she is sure has a better catch. Or in her lunch break she rushed over to Scaasi's, and there is the dearest little nothing for seven hundred and fifty that will simply make that second-act scene—and you have that scene pegged at a far cooler seventy-five, and she knows it. Or one of the actors just never could wear anything on his sensitive feet that wasn't custom made for him, and he wants a pair of boots that will only set the management back a little more than what he is getting a week. Or perhaps he really doesn't feel right coming back in the third act with the same old suit he wore in the second. It's keeping him from getting into the spirit of the thing. . . .

Stay out of these imbroglios if you want to stay in the theatre. You have an agreement to bring in this show at a certain figure, and part of your job is to try to stick to or under that amount. The ability to do this is part of your reputation. If it cannot be avoided, get the dissatisfied member of the company to ask for the larger expenditure himself. Often the business manager will be perfectly willing to be talked into additional expense by an old friend or favorite, and you will not be blamed for it. If, however, it is a change you want, then fight for it. But ordinarily, the actor can plead his own cause here better than you can.

But there are other problems you will hear about. The difficulties of sharing a dressing room with a mortal enemy—the one real laugh in the part given to another actor—lines cut and a small part dwindling because the show is running too long—the quick change in the middle of the second scene, and a need for a chance at the quick-change room, and a dresser (you make a personal note to see where the wardrobe woman is at that moment in the play). These and all the personal hurts, wounded vanities, and even private tragedies that cannot help but affect a performance . . . why are they telling you all this?

Because you are and you are not a member of the company. You are around often and long enough to know which laugh line is meant. The wardrobe, too, may have been pruned back with the cut lines. Proximity is part of it. You have probably spent hours with each member of the cast, in taxis, fitting rooms, or over a late cup of coffee, away from rehearsal, so it is safe to talk to you. And unless you have been seen to toady to that name that will be up in lights, or one of the understudies is known to be your dearest friend, by and large you are credited with impartiality. Try and hang on to that last quality. You will need it as much as any minister, doctor, or lawyer does. And like these last three, remember that the secrets of the fitting room are comparable to those of the confessional, for your ears alone. Talebearing, too much "So he said . . ." or "She told me . . ." can really make a tempestuous teapot out of a theatre. As it says in *Macbeth,* "Beware!"

On the other hand, there is a lot you can do. Sometimes just to be an audience will suffice. Listening is highly therapeutic. And some people can determine a course of action for themselves as they review the situation in telling it to someone else. Saying it aloud to someone whom the speaker is trying to convince will often help establish a fair point of view. Meanwhile, the costumer is beginning to feel like the Eyes and Ears of the World.

Sometimes you can help with a dropped hint to the stage manager, or some small ego builder of your own. But resist the temptation to become a therapist. Walk very softly, and be sure the stick you carry is no bigger than, say, the ferrule of a parasol.

Management often makes no bones about using you as a go-between. The producer may come to rehearsal and slip into the seat next to yours for a full three silent minutes. Then, after the ice has been broken, he will deliver himself of "Say, better tell that Sybil woman to get a tighter bra." Or "Tell his nibs that the seat of his trousers bags like an empty pillowcase." (The trousers are his nibs's own, since he is the star.) Or "I thought she said she was going to lose twenty-five pounds before rehearsal started. Tell her she better make it fifty!" And business accomplished, he walks away.

The last example is not as farfetched as you might think. It happens among the nonprofessionals too. When the actress refuses to tell the costume designer what she weighs, she is only acting like an ostrich. After a few years in the business, most designers could qualify as Coney Island weight guessers.

Make your own mental estimate, keep the answer to yourself, and when she says, "I always lose weight during rehearsals, so fit the clothes tight for now. I'll be inches smaller when we open . . ." just say, "Yes, dear," and prepare to keep on letting out seams.

This theory about losing during rehearsals is widespread, and from the fact that meals are irregular, hours possibly longer than in nonactive periods, and they are on their feet, working hard . . . well, they are also working up appetites. Sure, the meals are irregular, but they are usually sandwiches, the most fattening things ever, and they are frequent, what with coffee breaks with doughnuts or Danishes every few hours. And as soon as rehearsals are over, everyone troops to Sardi's or Downey's for the hot meal of the day. They have a couple of cocktails, to unwind, with a little beer to wash down the cannelloni, and then the lady goes home in a taxi to fall into bed and sleep, which is the most fattening way to digest a meal ever invented. If she loses weight during this regimen, she deserves a special Tony award.

I had one actress who tried to keep me with her most of the day and always wanted me to be the one she went out with after rehearsal. It wasn't my charm, she was terrified of my extra height and positive manner. She was also afraid to let me see her eating—she had made one of those promises. It got so I was even arriving at her apartment in time to supervise breakfast. And when one of the handsome actors in the company started taking up her free time, I groaned and started letting out seams. I knew training was going to be broken, and it was. This tall, thin actor got hungry and always wanted to eat after rehearsal, and he couldn't eat or drink alone. It would have made him seem alcoholic.

Then there was the actress who ate to compensate. She was breaking up with her husband, and since it was her fourth, she thought she ought to hang on to him. And there was the actress who thought all overweight was water retention, and that the way to lose pounds was to cut all the water from her diet, just drink her bourbon on the rocks. She nearly fixed her kidneys, and herself, with that theory, and she was only saved from a physical breakdown when the doctor she went to for a diuretic shot spotted what her trouble was and got her to bed with a lot of water and some kidney medication.

The only way to lose weight is to take the world's best exercise—push yourself away from the table, even if you *think* you are still hungry. And to keep it off, repeat the same exercise indefinitely.

Anyone who thinks all this involvement doesn't make you a member of the company is crazy. Men have been given Lambs or Players membership for far less.

Why go on? Anybody can finish these stories for himself.

You may hear about the wardrobe woman's objection to having to stitch a tablecloth for props. You may hear about an actor who needs an operation, but who is trying to hold out until after the opening, so please don't tell anybody. And sitting in the dark there watching rehearsals, you may hear quite a lot from that restless person who has been pacing around at the back and who finally sinks into the vacant seat beside you and uses you as a safety valve—the author, who cannot stand the way an actor reads a certain line—the director, who thinks the whole third scene needs rewriting, but no one agrees with him—even the scene designer, who is worried about whether that French door is going to stand up under the not too skillful ministrations of the man who plays the butler. What you will do about this kind of confidence depends upon the kind of person you are, and I cannot advise you. I can only warn you that the situation may arise.

Occasionally you will hear tales that strike a deeper note, approaching the drama of the play itself. There is the older actress who has only taken the part—which is too strenuous for her—to support an even older husband in the hospital. There is the assistant stage manager also doing a walk-on, whose young wife is expecting her first baby sometime during the three weeks the play will be opening in Toronto. What you can say to or do for these people is a matter of your own personality.

What we are examining now is why the costume designer becomes involved in these confidences. Is it the designer himself who invites them or is it something that comes with the job? I think it is a little of both. Certainly there are some designers in whom a sane actor would not confide the time of day. And there are others who immediately inspire the company to reveal—oh, the least dwindling digit of a personal checking account. Being a member of Local 829 does not alter your status as a human being, and you will have people coming to you just as you always have. But what is there about the job itself that creates this situation?

Possibly there is the feeling that since you already know so much, there is little to be feared. Having revealed the most secret secrets—the number of inches to a waistline or the exact size of a shoe—they make you privy to the rest. Begin by telling someone the worst about yourself, and it is not unusual to feel safe letting him in on some of the lighter portions of your existence.

Part of it is the actor's natural tendency to talk, preferably about himself. It is part of what makes him an actor, his outgoing egocentricity. I cannot recollect meeting one who was taciturn or nontalkative. And the actor cannot talk as much to other members of the cast—they are all actors. As such, they would demand equal time on the program.

Another reason for the alliance between the designer and the actors has already been mentioned—proximity. It is not your business to sit around management's offices, listening to the bull sessions going on there. But it is your business to spend as much time as you can spare from your outside work at rehearsals, watching the progress of the play.

A final point to be considered is the actual nature of your work. Just as the actor is creative, so is the designer. Their basic characteristics draw them together. It is the old birds-of-a-feather business. Actors and designers come closer to having a common language with each other than with management, so that there is more chance of an understanding. Think, too, of the actor's personality. That same quality that is going to be operating behind footlights after the curtain goes up is probably being used on you in small doses by way of a practice performance. If you find yourself responding to a famous actor or actress in the same dedicated way that thousands in audiences have, that does not mean that you are a tool or a dupe. It simply means that you have encountered a member of Actors' Equity who has the elements of his profession at his fingertips and can twist you around them. It's fun to be fooled.

Just remember that most of these I-wants are not always life or death matters. Remember, too, to avoid becoming a gossip by betraying a confidence. That could cost you your next job with the same organization. Then go ahead and don't belabor yourself if in the process of working you find yourself on the side of the actors, not the side of the angels.

8

⌒⌒

The Out-of-Town Tryout

The best way to go to an out-of-town tryout is in a chauffeur-driven car. I did it just once, thanks to a friend who had to return a borrowed car to the Boston area, and the luxury of it all was indescribable. There was room for everything I had to take along—last minute deliveries of shoes, hats, wigs, an evening dress and bulky wrap, plus all those precious items I didn't dare trust to anyone else, such as some borrowed real jewelry. To top it all, I slept all the way up, and it seems to me those five lovely hours totaled more time with my eyes closed than I had managed consecutively for weeks.

Failing this, normal procedure is to travel by train in the company car, usually reserved just for the use of the producer's people. This is usually fun, for that train trip to Boston, or New Haven or Washington or Wilmington, is the high road to adventure, the primrose path of the gambler

that may end with the long shot romping in ahead of the
field, or in a discouraging failure. But most theatre people
are gamblers, whether they will admit it or not, and at this
point your money is still as good as the other fellow's, even
if his name is Merrick and he's going to open against you on
the same street with more advance publicity. You will probably feel this way, too, unless you are wondering why the
wardrobe box count shows only twelve pair of gauntlets instead of the fifteen you had specified.

It would also be nice if you are traveling with a confirmed
hotel reservation. In this area the designer is the forgotten
man, or woman. When reservations are being made, management tends to think of the designer as a member of the
company, which means that the stage manager will have
him on *his* list, and the stage manager knows perfectly well
the designer is part of management and therefore gets taken
care of by the office. Unless you are addicted to sleeping on a
banquet table in the deserted hotel ballroom, or curled up
among the pin trays and clothes hangers in the theatre wardrobe room, I suggest you check this out thoroughly before
leaving the safety of your New York apartment. The only
member of the company who will turn out to have engaged
a room with an unoccupied twin bed will be, I can almost
promise you, a member of the opposite sex. . . .

Leave your own things, if you can separate them from
the play material, at your hotel, take a last loving look at
the room you will probably not see again for hours and
hours, gaze fondly at the bed and think of how all the actors
are curling up on similar beds for an hour or two nap until

the first call, and then run all the way to the theatre. If it is the DuPont Playhouse in Wilmington you are in luck; you only have to take the elevator to the lobby and walk a covered half block, past, if you avert your eyes, a cocktail bar from which comes the throaty voice of the character actress saying "Cheers" to the dashing juvenile. Resolutely make your way to the theatre, find the wardrobe room by climbing under masses of unanchored electrical wiring and crawling through tunnels of unloaded scenery and furniture, and see if the wardrobe woman is there, and if she is unpacking and pressing the costumes.

No one is allowed to unpack the wardrobe trunks except your union wardrobe woman, and her assistant. She will probably have already arranged for an assistant from the local union to help with this, which seems to be legal even when there are only three costumes for the whole show. In an extreme emergency, you yourself are permitted to open that Pandora's box, but I suggest hands off if possible. Anyway, next order of the day is to press the clothes and distribute them in the proper dressing rooms in the proper order for their appearance.

One of the most useful things you can have done for yourself at this point is to have prepared four copies of a list that details every item of every costume as it should appear onstage—one to the stage manager, one to the wardrobe mistress, one to the actor or actors, and keep one for yourself.

For example:

WARDROBE—MISS SARAH STARR

Entrance:

Red dress. Belt. Brown calf pumps. Brown bag. Fur stole. Pearl necklace, earrings, and ring. Pearl clip on dress.

First change: 2-1

Blue negligee. No hose. Blue satin mules. No jewels except pearl ring. Ribbon, blue, in hair.

Second change: 2-2

White slip over girdle and bra. Hose. White satin pumps. Wig for last act elaborate coiffure. Jewels same.

Third change: 3-1

Wedding gown. Veil and wreath. Pearl necklace. White kid gloves. Chantilly lace fan. Bouquet.

WARDROBE—SIR LAWRENCE LEAD

Open: -1-

Entrance: 1-1

Gray flannel trousers. Handkerchief in left rear pocket. White button-down shirt open at neck, sleeves rolled. No tie. Black socks, no garters. Sneakers. Painter's cap on head. Wristwatch. Dog-tag chain at neck.

First change: 2-1

Shirt, trousers, socks, same as above, but with sleeves down, garters added. Street shoes. Green tie, tiepin. Jacket of suit. Breast pocket handkerchief. Wallet in inside pocket. Carry snap-brim hat.

Second change: 3-1

Striped trousers, oxford-gray morning jacket. Pleated-bosom shirt, cuff links and matching tiepin. Black satin tie. White handkerchief in breast pocket. Black socks. Dress shoes. Homburg hat. Gloves. Carnation in buttonhole.

FROM PROP TABLE: Bamboo-handled umbrella.

WARDROBE—GEORGE SPELVIN

Entrance: 3-3

Policeman's uniform. Trousers, shirt, jacket. Socks, shoes, tie, hat, belt. Holster and revolver. Cartridge case. Badge.

PROP TABLE: Book of tickets.

The above list is not mandatory, unless the stage manager is of that rare breed who requests it. But all you have to do is open one show with any costume changes at all to see that it certainly is salutary.

The first day of the company's arrival out of town, it will probably not be possible to use the stage. It will be in a fine state of confusion, the set unassembled, stagehands all over the place, and often with an electrical switchboard to be moved into some as yet undetermined place. There will not be room for a six-week-old runt-sized kitten, and so the director is most likely to call for a line rehearsal, in the auditorium, the Green Room, or even the producer's suite at the hotel. This, if you are still able to maintain an upright position, will give you time to get some of your own work done. Or it is, possibly, the last time you will have for weeks to see a hairdresser.

If you can safely leave the wardrobe women to unpack, press, and distribute the clothes in the proper dressing rooms, the best thing I have ever done is to go out and case the town. If you have never been there before, this is important. Even if you have spent weekends there for the good Old Woonsockie football game the last few years, you are now going out to find another side. Instead of the best bar that is open late or the finest steamed clams or soft shell crabs, what you now want is the exact location of the biggest and juiciest five-and-ten. Also try to find out where to buy a pair of workman's boots or a chef's hat if you are likely to need them, the most complete and well-stocked department store in town, a good and close shoe-repair place, preferably one that is open till all hours and that will dye shoes, and a tailor shop that can be trusted to do alterations— even re-creations—on men's suits. Hopefully, you won't need any of this nonsense. You are probably much more efficient than I was. But just in case you do, it makes you sound awfully good to the wardrobe woman when you can tell her that on the corner of Spruce and Walnut there's a little shoe shop where they'll dye those pink shoes blue overnight.

The business of scuffing up the too-new soles of shoes is not difficult, if you can generate enough friction. In *Gently Does It* we had a pair of riding boots worn by an actress who was supposed to be an addicted horsewoman, but from rows A and AA the bottoms of her boots had obviously never seen a stirrup, and she must have been lifted onto a horse not from the ground, but from the sill of a living room that had wall-to-wall carpeting. The boots had had five polishings to soften and break down the uppers, but the shoeshine boy must have kept the soles on white satin as he worked.

Just wearing them around the theatre for the twenty-four hours we had left was not going to do it as could be seen at the end of an hour. Scuffing shoes on the sidewalk in front of the theatre hardly seemed the best way of advertising the play to the people standing in line in front of the box office, a line I saw when I went out the front of the house, boots under my arm. Shuffling dejectedly back to reenter the theatre by the stage door, I saw one of the happiest sights I could have imagined—the side of the alley to the stage was composed, on my right, of very rough, common, discolored, and dirty old red brick. Putting one boot on each of my hands I started climbing that wall, up and down, over and over, singing happily, "Yankee Doodle went to town, riding on a pony . . ." I'd have worn a feather in my cap for all I cared what I looked like.

Spraying, painting, and other forms of artificial aging are all very well, but there is nothing like real, genuine dirt for making things look dirty. We had reached Boston on a tryout tour when I had to buy Mel Douglas a new pair of gray flannel slacks and make them look as if he had worn them while being dragged across a full-length football field.

Boston is complete with a large collection of good men's shops, and it was no later than eleven in the morning when I arrived backstage with the slacks neatly folded in a distinguished haberdasher's box. The wardrobe steam iron took care of removing the creases, an operation so against the grain for me as to seem vandalism, but I did it. Next, the dirt. The stage had been swept and dusted for the evening's performance. I have never seen a backstage so immaculate before or since. I was moping around trying to find even one speck when the stage manager caught me. "I know," he said, "Boston Common." He also insisted on doing the job for me, for which I can never thank him enough.

It was about high noon when he invaded the Common, and he was almost in among the swans before he found what he wanted, a gravel path old fashioned enough to have dirt, stones, twigs, and all those homey comforts. Taking off his jacket he laid it carefully in the chic box and removing the slacks he went to work. Bruce had hardly given the antique finish to one trouser leg when he looked up to find a policeman standing over him. "Say, young fella, what the devil do you think you're doing? You crazy or somethin'?"

Bruce tried to explain, but it didn't make sense to the Boston protector of law and order. This was so disorderly as to seem like nutty behavior to him, and he was all for calling in reinforcements that would have padded walls and a straightjacket handy. It took fast talking from the stage manager to persuade the officer to accompany him back to the theatre to check out the story. Scooping up a last handful of dirt, which he put into his own pocket for the other trouser leg, Bruce proceeded back to the theatre, looking as if he were already under arrest.

That policeman tailed his suspect back to the theatre, where I tried to confirm his allegations. But there was circumstantial evidence against him, and my story was regarded as hearsay. Apparently seeing is believing. That officer ended up with two free tickets for the Boston opening of *Time Out for Ginger,* which ran over a year in New York, sent out a national company, and was made into a movie.

When the director and cast have made a partial reconquest of the proscenium area, and the set designer and lighting expert will grant them a few, brief, interrupted hours to work there, like from two to seven-thirty A.M., the schedule will usually run like this: First day, furniture and prop rehearsal. Dress parade, which is not the same as a dress rehearsal. The actors won't wear their costumes to work in, or may not even put them on in proper sequence. Miss Starr may walk to the footlights to show the producer and director her third-act change while the ingenue is pivoting around in the thin ice-skating costume she wears in the opening scene. But for your own sake, if nobody else's, try to get a look at things in the set that will be worn at the same time. It's very nice to know what goes with what, and if it really does.

Next day, and as many days as remain before the opening, there will be dress rehearsals. Get as many as you can. You learn something, usually disastrous, every time.

If you haven't already formed the addiction, here's where a lighted clipboard will start working its way through your bloodstream and toward your heart. Just try keeping these important notes in order when you've written them in a black theatre, in a hurry, and even possibly in a panic. This helpful tool has a battery-powered light on the clip, shaded to fall just where you write, and can be bought or ordered through most of the good stationery supply houses. The aluminum ones are best, lightest, and most expensive.

By now, too, your pockets, or pocketbook, should be brimming with the real essentials. Keep your eyeglasses and your cigarettes, but, if you need the space, throw away your Diners' Club card, that letter from home, even your wallet, and be sure to carry a small pair of scissors, a paper of pins, needle, thimble, thread, some safety pins, and anything else you can think of that will make things either stick together or come apart quickly. If you're the kind who's never been able to sew a button in place to stay, perhaps you'd better drop this course. . . . Or should I have brought that up earlier?

One other item for that vest-pocket list of necessities— aspirin. Perhaps you never take it, though your first dress rehearsal might cause you to change. But even if you don't, probably half the acting company does, and you might find that a few hundred tablets tucked somewhere handy will make you look better than a whole litter of Saint Bernards complete with brandy casks.

Perhaps this is beginning to sound like a deliberate setting out with desert island equipment. But there will be times during the preopening period when the theatre will be like a desert island, late at night, always on Sundays. It never keeps store hours, and there are times when you'd give anything for a cigarette or a cup of coffee, but there just isn't anybody around to take your money.

What can I tell you about a dress rehearsal if you've never been to one? There are no two alike, since each one is a composite of all the different elements that go to make up the play itself. Not just your costumes, but the theatre, the scenery, the director, the ability and preparedness of the actors, the craftswomanship of your wardrobe mistress, even

whether the theatre owner is being chintzy about the heat
will make a difference. It is not even possible to say when it
will start, or end. In spite of the unions, here's where rules
fly out the stage door. But end it will, so just sit tight, trying
to keep control of yourself and your notes. Try to see everything, not just the main facets, such as how a particular outfit looks under lights, but whether the ingenue's petticoat
shows and if the character actress needs more color in her
foundation makeup. Do you suddenly find that that handbag
of the heroine is going to have to be replaced by one with
a strap, for easier handling, and what about the underside
of all the shoes? Do they all look as if, which is true, of
course, they'd never seen an honest pavement in all their un-
born-calf days?

One more thing—try to see each group of costumes from
each of the various main sections of the theatre. Front row,
back row, all around the house. Distance may lend enchant-
ment, or make a serious difference, and the paying customers
don't all sit, as you may have been doing, in the first ten
rows.

Now, unless you have been wizard enough to pull off a
dress rehearsal with no corrections to be made, one of the
most difficult parts of Operation Theatre begins. Actors'
Equity, the actors' union, requires that a rehearsal call can't
be issued until twelve hours after the curtain has gone down
on the last one. So the weary actors stagger home for some
well-deserved rest. You, who deserve it just as much, probably must function like the famous goblins in the shoemaker's
fairy tale—you work while they sleep. That long list of things

to do must be done in time for the next dress rehearsal, or, if that's the schedule, the opening. Of course if it's shoes you need, or anti-radiation masks, you can give yourself until the stores open. But, looking at the sky it's ten to one you will say, "If dawn is here, can day be far behind?"

Grab the two, three, four hours of sleep you can allow yourself, probably fully clothed on top of your bed. Fortunately the coffeehouses are early openers.

By eleven, or one, or whenever the call is, you should, if it is humanly possible, have completed everything on last night's list. This is not only part of your job, it is also self-defense. Tonight's list is apt to be just as long. If the director, producer, and author can't think of a single other thing to do to the play at this stage, it could even be longer. They must have it as one of the secret rules of their association— if there's nothing else you can think of to do to the play, try fiddling with the costumes.

When the notices come out the morning after the opening, you may have a brief respite. The out-of-town critics don't pay much attention to the clothes, except in unusual circumstances. But the play and the performances are apt to get a fair share of clobbering, which will keep everybody busy and give you time to get those hems that were just basted done properly. But don't make the sad mistake of relaxing too much and letting your muscles go slack. Now is when actors are replaced, and they will fly that new one on from the Coast without first finding out whether he can wear that forty-six portly that fitted actor number one. A serious re-write may also produce a serious change in the costumes as serendipity. So just stay prepared for anything.

One thing may, at this point, be a consolation to you. You can hope that, as in one of the old superstitions of the theatre, a bad dress rehearsal means a good opening, a bad out-of-town opening may mean a good New York opening.

9

The Period of Bereavement

After the Broadway opening—what?

Well, first off, the next morning you drag yourself up out of bed, which probably seems the most desirable spot in the whole world, and make for the reviews in the morning papers. Very few of them are going to mention the wardrobe, but it might be nice to know what those six good men and true think about the actors and if it is at all likely the play is to be a hit. Then you go back to bed to wait for Wednesday, with its appearance of *Variety*.

This paper is worth waiting for, since it not only gives an estimate of the potential box office but is apt at least to mention the wardrobe, even when the production is not one that concentrates on clothes. The other one to look for, and which does not pretend that, for all of it, the actors went on in the nude, is *Women's Wear Daily*, which does a fairly good review on the play itself, along with mentioning the wearing apparel. Those buyers from out of town are part of the carriage trade at any hit.

If it just so happens that the *Times* man has picked up a discordant dressing note, such as the fact that the comedienne went on, on opening night, wearing one red and one black shoe, you will want to rush backstage to rectify your reasoning. Also, in the press of the premiere, there may be a few things still to be done, such as getting the final really finished third underpetticoat together with the costume, but by and large, for the next few days, there is nothing much for you to do, except catch up on that terribly neglected sleep and answer congratulatory telegrams.

Now begins the bad part. Some writers have what they call the Period of Bereavement after they finish a book. They feel they have struggled for months, pregnant with book, and at last have given birth. But unlike other parents, who can keep busy and distracted with the care and feeding of the infant, the author is beset by an aura of gloom and despondency as if his little darling had been DOA.

The costume designer is very apt to find himself in this same moribund atmosphere. For weeks he has been working, likely more than the usual eight hours a day, certainly more than the writer's occasional three, four, or five. His whole life has been focused on getting his balloon into the air and off the ground, often to the exclusion of friends, food, and biannual trips to the dentist. By now his toothache has stopped, his friends have gone away mad, and he has forgotten that some folk eat regular meals, at appointed and sociable hours. He has nothing to do with himself, his life is an empty theatre.

There are a few things you can do to help yourself up out of this morass. First, give a party for your friends. I do not mean that old Equity crowd, but the other people you used to know whose lives are not bounded by the Ziegfeld on the north, where the old Empire used to be on the south, the Martin Beck on the west, and the Hudson on the east. Some of these friends, except for your inner circle, may not even know you have been designing a Broadway show. Fame is like that. But you can tell them, and if the show is a hit, that will be fun. (But be careful to avoid getting into the position where they ask you for seats. Make it clear that the line forms at the box office, not on your memo pad. Costume designers do not get house seats, and even these, when available, have to be paid for. I have one actress friend who gets her arm twisted this way for at least one-tenth of her salary.)

Though it may be hard to overcome the habits of weeks, try to remember that standard fare for this party is not coffee in leaky paper cups and sandwiches wrapped in wax paper and served in paper bags. You might even enjoy thinking of some good hot food for a change, and whip up a noble roast of beef, *hot* rolls, and a superlative salad. Besides, better be nice to these people. If you never get another job, they may have to feed *you* for more than one evening.

Then, after the show has been running a couple of weeks, you can begin a mild form of riding herd on your creations. But be careful not to overdo, or everyone, beginning with the wardrobe woman, will hate you. And if she hates you, she can sabotage your costuming now that you are away from the theatre.

But you do have every right to check on the appearance

of the costumes after a couple of weeks of eight performances a week and some quick changes. So if the stage doorman still remembers who you are, which is unlikely, or if the company or stage or business manager will arrange to let you in—you may have to stand in the back—go down to look things over.

See if the things are going out to a theatrical cleaner often enough to stay fresh and new looking. Caution: Don't over-clean either, it wears clothes out.

See if any actress has put her heel through a hem and has a sagging skirt line, or if slips have started to show. This is properly the wardrobe woman's responsibility, and if she is good, you can relax and forget about it after one check.

See that the actors themselves have not redesigned the costuming while your back was turned. Maybe someone has gone back to wearing a hat that was discarded in New Haven but that she really liked much better than the more recent selection in which she opened. Maybe it's too much trouble to put on all that jewelry, especially since the weather has turned so hot. Perhaps someone has taken to appearing in an old pair of his own shoes. Yes, he knows they are the wrong period, but they are so much more comfortable. The others were giving him corns. . . .

If it is something you think is actually bad, and it matters, raise a fuss about it. Nobody has the right to change your costuming without your permission, not even the producer. And if necessary, the union will back you up on this, particularly if the fight *is* with the producer.

One of the arduous chores you will have to attend to is to provide the office with the final version of the budget, all paid up and completed. Or, if your arrangements are that way, showing what bills are paid, and exactly how much is still outstanding. The producer needs this, because until it is in his hands he can make no final and irrefutable estimate of the cost of the production. This must go to the backers as soon as possible. Also, cost of production is figured separately from running costs, and repayment of the financing needs the inclusion of these balances to be figured properly. This is tedious work for you, since it must include every package of pins or pair of dress shields, unless you wish to make these voluntary offerings out of your own pocket on the altar of Thespis. If you have been smart and provident, you will have kept a daily score sheet that will mean you are almost up to date, but it may take several productions before you learn how it pays in the long run to *be* smart and provident.

If everybody is pleased with your work, your financial acumen, and the show is a hit, there is always the national company to look forward to. This used to be called Going on the Road, or the touring company, but we have gotten more elegant about it in the last decade. Elegant or not, this company does not usually take off until the original Broadway version has been running on the Big Stem for about a year, so it is not worth sitting home waiting for the phone to ring for about the first ten or eleven months.

What you need now is to get another job. To return to those writers and their bereavement, it is easier for them than for a designer. All the writer needs is his typewriter, any old kind of paper, and an Idea, and he can cure his own broken heart. *You* need an employer. In most cases these are as hard to come by as a good playscript.

For the way to find that employer, I refer you to the earlier chapter, How to Get That First Job. By now, of course, you have one added asset—Broadway experience.

Of all the contributors to the Seven Lively Arts, the writers and the painters have a distinct advantage. They can function on their own. They do not need to be employed to get the satisfaction that comes from work, nor do they require an audience. Musicians need other performers, such as singers, or a symphony. The actor is, it seems to me, the most frustrated—he not only needs the attentive theatreful, he needs fellow actors to read the other lines. One cannot make a satisfactory, satisfying career out of doing the *Hamlet* soliloquy in one's fifth floor walk-up bed-sitting room, and a tape recorder is so unresponsive. An audience gives back to the actor something he can set his teeth in, or against.

Once the author is past the first beginning hurdle, page or paragraph as the case may be, he can go it alone. In fact, it is essential to go it alone, for some. But the costume designer is in the dependent group. Like the actor, he too needs a theatre in which to perform. But his cure for the aches and pains is still the same in this period of bereavement. Get back to work.

If you can have a second occupation it is a help. Some costumers make excellent interior decorators. Their sense of color and the showmanship they develop are distinct assets. Some designers have private dressmaking businesses, even up to the couture level. Or, of course, you could always try to write a play.

10

The Cretonne-Covered Couch

One of the first things the designer needs to begin work on a play is, as I've mentioned, a consultation with the set designer. From this consultation he must emerge with one of his primary objectives—color chips and fabric swatches of the background against which his own part of the drama will be played.

This is not always as simple as it sounds. The samples are not in this office, they are over at the studio where the set is being built. Or there just aren't any swatches of the drapery material, the last one went to the mill at Worcester with a reorder—imagine, they were three and a quarter yards short! No, there aren't any color chips of the wall color. What do you need a chip of that for? It's just plain beige. Well, you do need that color reference, so hang on grimly until you get it, or go over to the construction studio and get one for yourself on a piece of heavy drawing paper, a bit of wood, or on your right sleeve, if necessary.

Try, if it is possible, to get a look at some version of the design itself. At Jo Mielziner's, you may see an exact little mock-up of the set, with movable parts. George Jenkins, on the other hand, will show you a watercolor rendering that is so beautiful you will want to take it home and frame it. Some other designer may just have left the fool thing in the pocket of his other suit, and will describe it for you, with illustrative flourishes of his hands. Whatever it is, pay attention. This is in the same relation to the work you will do as that crinkled satin that lines the inside of the box displaying the forty-eight-piece silver service, or that small square of black velvet onto which the Fifth Avenue jeweler casually tosses the fifty-thousand-dollar bracelet. It is the background against which you and your own work must shine forth, and it can either make it easy for you, or break you.

The scene designer is, in a sense, the superior of the costume designer. He was hired before the latter, and he gets more money. He deserves this, since his work requires greater knowledge. He must be both architect and carpenter, in addition to being an artist. Also, his is the "parent" body in the union, so his is the ranking position here, too. But unless the contract so stipulates, he is not your boss. He can control, to a certain extent, by his previously selected forms and colors, what you do, but he cannot *tell* you what to do. Neither can you tell him, of course, that you don't want him to use gray walls, since you are planning a gray cape. . . .

In one area, however, your actual working position is superior to his. You are much more closely related to the actor. The set designer's chief field of influence is with the director. His control over the working out of the play is in the fact that his picture sets the mood for the play at the moment that the curtain rises, and his control is always maintained, to a certain extent, by the fact that he has allocated the physical boundaries of playing areas. And your own control, and contribution to the play, by reason of its immediate effect on the physical appearance of the actor himself, is a very vital and continuing one in that playing field. And because, with every costume change during the play, you have the opportunity to maintain, improve, or even change, the effect of what you are doing, your own sphere of influence in the theatre is functioning right up to the final curtain. So don't disparage yourself.

Even the bare stage *Hamlet* doesn't play it bare-assed. While the actor may pay no attention to the fact that the wall behind him is a brick one strung with pipes and light cords, he is probably going to care more about what he will wear. You can play the prince of Denmark in modern dress, but it should not be a pin-striped double-breasted suit. And he may need a designer to suggest to him that narrow black trousers, a black knit shirt open at the neck but with long sleeves, would be much more appropriate. Register the royalty with a fine alligator belt with a gold buckle—and, oh yes, let his hair grow another half inch longer. Shoes? A soft, dark desert boot or moccasin.

The scene designer—and it is almost safe to bet on this —has designed his picture as a whole. Think back to that beautiful sketch or that lovely mock-up. Do they need people, or aren't they complete in themselves, like Cézanne's still life of apples, or the Van Gogh of a bed, a window, and a chair? You are going to be in the position of having to set a mouse to nibble at those apples, or tossing a figure across that empty bed. And what you do not want is to make a collage out of a painting with scraps of fabric pasted onto the surface. Depending on the play, your people must merge with and emerge from the background as if it were their native habitat, which it is supposed to be for two and a half hours, or stand out against it, in sharp protest as the author intends them to fight against their environment for the duration of his play.

To illustrate how the costumer must work, let us take the first situation. It is easier to use as an example. Say that the set is a living room, and the home of most of the characters. They are people of good, if not excessive taste, so they are not likely to appear in clothing that is an affront to their surroundings—except possibly for a purpose. But neither did they buy their garments with an eye to how they would look when they walked through their house; they are not that studied or self-conscious about their wearing apparel. But you are, you must be. And here is where your own use of dramatic license is called into play.

Now you need those color chips and swatches. Spread them out in front of you and study them. The walls are to be a soft green, about the color of an olive. Good, that's an easy color off which to refract costumes. But there's a contrasting molding of creamy white! You can understand why; the designer wants the effect of a crowded room, and all those framed doorways and windows with the molded contrasts will help give that. . . . Draperies are a stripe, green, mulberry, and the off-white, about two inches wide. One chair repeats the stripe, one is solid mulberry. One chair in a woven damask so small it comes out a neutral—that's a help. But the couch fabric is a cretonne, with every color in the room and then some, in it. And the couch is dead center stage, just as the author ordered, and everybody and his brother are going to sit on it. And the flowers and pheasants in the cretonne are all life size or better!

Chair here, there, occasional tables here and here, and desk there. But these are all wood, stained mahogany, and don't have to be worried over. Wood, bless it, goes with everything. Lampshades gold, and so is the desk chair, but the former too small to be considered, and when anyone sits in that chair, its upholstered area is so small that it will be completely covered by the occupant. . . . Rug? Murder! A patterned Brussels with every color in the rainbow, in spades. Unless there's a raked stage that slants upward to the back, the carriage trade will never know about it. But all those people in the mezzanine and balcony are going to be staring down at it for three acts, and they did pay money for their tickets, too. So, take the rug into consideration.

Winding up, there's a corner cupboard with the inside painted indigo—of all colors—and a breakfront with a toile curtain in green and white. What with the metallic lattice, forget about the breakfront, it comes out as a neutral again, but what about that corner cupboard? Where is it placed, and how much action takes place in front of it? See script.

In fact, now look at the script to see if you can roughly determine what the playing areas will be, how important each of these color commitments will be in relation to the clothes. You can't tell where the director will choreograph the actual business of each character, but certain things are inevitable. The cretonne-covered couch looms large.

Referring to the script again, look for references to that couch. Placed as it is, and of the size that it is, it is obviously going to be a dominant factor. Even without knowing what specific action the director will dictate, the author has already committed some of the action. "Crosses to the couch" or "Drawing her legs up under her on the couch" gives you a rough idea.

Let us consider the couch, then, using it as a symbol. It works very well in this respect, placed centrally as it is, and figuring prominently in the action. There is an infinite variety of things you can play off against it. The main thing is to keep in mind the things you cannot do.

Suppose that the fabric contains a multitude of colors. From the viewpoint of costuming, this is an asset. Against that many colors you can bounce off almost any solid color you want—or need. But basically, what you have to remember is that it must be a solid color, no print or perceptible stripe. The only time you would use either of these would be when you want to create a deliberate effect of busyness, as with a restless and perhaps strident character. Even this is a little dangerous, for when you do it visibly, it can sometimes be so positive an effect as to set the teeth of the audience on edge. Do you want to do that? It is almost as risky a thing to do as when the author decides to write one of his characters in as an old bore. Unless he is magnificently adroit, the character will bore the audience instead of amusing them.

Decide on the types of wearing apparel that *cannot* sit on or stand in front of your couch and keep them in mind. Unless there is some specific reason for it, consider the actress's own preferences seriously. The more you hem her in with specified restrictions, the more you will hinder her performance. Actually, your job is to free her and help her create the character she is after by giving her clothing that is part of that character.

Incidentally, I say "actress" here because it is most frequently that you will have a conflict between the set and the women's clothes. Obviously, the same rules apply to men's wear.

What is true of the couch is also true, of course, of every major piece of furniture or color area—walls, draperies, etc., on the set. Your problem is to evaluate them and their position and see how they affect you. Some of them, though they may take a fair space on the set designer's chart of samples, may turn out to be less significant than they had seemed. That corner cupboard, for example, with the indigo shelves, may be so placed that it faces practically offstage. Or those sharp blue shelves may be almost blocked out by an array of pewter plates and tankards that would make a handsome foil for any dressing you could think up. Here you must use your own judgment. Or this color obstacle may be shunted off into what turns out not to be a playing area. Dropping in on rehearsals will settle this for you. Subject to change at the very last minute, naturally.

But before you walk away from that couch, one more thing. Is there a door other than the entrance, in any of the three walls that surround it? Does that door swing open, at any point in the play, to reveal a closet, gaping emptily. This, then, is what I call the skeletal closet. Its very existence can, if neglected, provide you with more minor horrors than All Hallows' Eve.

If at any portion of the play that door opens to show the inside of the closet, that closet must be "dressed." And if the door is there at all, chances are it's a practical one. They are rarely useful as ornamentation. They increase the cost of construction, and they destroy precious wall space. What shows inside is probably partly up to you. But aren't those things props? Only yes and no.

The suitcases, tennis rackets, piles of magazines, and the folding chairs are props, and the business of the man in charge of that department. But the raincoats, galoshes, mackintoshes, and the old kitchen apron are your department, even if the actors don't come within a measured mile of wearing any of them. I've even had to provide the paper hatboxes with the name of my favorite millinery designer on them, on the propman's insistence that it was woman's work. So though I got those boxes from Mrs. V, I hightailed it to a thrift shop or a rummage sale for the balance of the furnishings. It's wonderful what you can acquire for fifty cents or a dollar that is absolutely great, as long as nobody is going to wear it. Here is one of those places where you can amuse yourself being imaginative about what the well-dressed closet will contain.

Unless, of course, they want that closet lined with diamond-studded mink.

There are all kinds of couches in a costume designer's life. There is the beat-up, broken-springed one that serves as a small boy's bed in a drab Harlem apartment, or the simple army cot with a flowered bedspread thrown on top. There will be gay sets, like Mr. Mielziner's—this couch in purple, the chairs chartreuse, the walls magenta. Or the perfect austerity and good taste of a George Jenkins living room, done with fine wood period pieces against which any clothes should look well. Or Eldon Elder's comfortably cluttered family room, with a football playing field for the central area. Or Pat Campbell's working girl's housekeeping one room, complete with Castro convertible and an ironing board perpetually in use. . . .

There's a problem in every one of them, naturally, but an invitation to ingenuity too. One learns to cope, though it seems difficult at times. You have to. Otherwise you'll find yourself not staring at that couch, but on one, leather-covered, in some doctor's office. And it would be perfectly reasonable, to me at least, for you to worry, as you lie down, if you are wearing the right thing.

11

What Color Should a Heroine Wear?

In the last twenty-five years we have seen many things that were just theories develop into sciences. In view of so much enlightenment it is a shame that one of the most influential of these theories, the science of color, should have advanced so slowly. Actually color is one of the most *affective* of our daily influences and it should not be allowed to affect us, to operate on us, on such a hit-or-miss basis. When the effect of color on people (their reaction to it) is strong enough to determine the cut of meat they buy at the supermarket, agitate a patient waiting in a dentist's office, or make one dislike on sight that thoroughly nice woman one has just met simply because she is wearing an orange hat, one would think the time had come to make use of color to achieve the goals we work for. But actually the science of color is still in its infancy and, to make it even worse, few people begin to use the little we do know about it.

There is always the possibility that as these lines are being written someone is putting the final period at the end of a new study of color. Let us hope so. For anyone really interested in what can be done along these lines I recommend a trip to the bookstore or library to inquire into the newest work on the subject. At the present moment I cannot give you any worthwhile bibliography and though at one point I read everything on which I could lay my hands, compared with what I would like to know about the psychological uses of color what will appear here can only cover these pages with a very thin watercolor wash. Sorry.

So, taking with us the small amounts of ammunition we do have, let us proceed, upstream as it is, into this largely uncharted territory. There are a few things we do know, though they are pretty much in the two-plus-two-makes-four category.

Most people have studied at least the rudiments of a color system, but it might be wise to run through a quick refresher here. There are three primary colors—*red, blue,* and *yellow* —and three secondary ones—*green, orange,* and *violet*. White and black are not colors but rather the absence of all color and the presence of all color respectively—though they must be considered as colors in the business of costume design.

There are two kinds of color that concern the designer, complementary and analogous. To best explain these, let us confine the color range in a circle—harness it into a clock-face, to be exact. We are going to put twelve colors into that clock, one for each of the spaces usually taken up by the hours on the dial. Starting at high noon, the first color is red.

Moving clockwise around the circle, the next color, at one o'clock, will be red-orange. Next comes orange, then yellow-orange, then yellow. Now we are at four o'clock. Then comes yellow-green, green at six, blue-green, blue at eight, blue-violet, violet, red-violet and back to red on the stroke of twelve, just where we left it. Or has something about this color clock escaped you?

There are three primary colors: red, yellow, and blue. On our imaginary clockface, they appear at twelve, four, and eight. With these colors we can make any one color on the palette if we have them in a pure enough form, such as in a pure paint, a light, or an aniline dye. (All three colors together, for instance, make brown.)

Each color has its opposite or complementary color. I imagine the term comes from the fact that any color, with its complement, involves the full range of the primary, or basic pigments. Take a simple example: the complement to red is green, made by a mixture of the two other primaries, yellow and blue. The elements of this hold true all around the spectrum. On our imaginary color wheel, draw a diagonal from any color, passing through the center, to the color opposite it. This will be its complementary color. For instance, start with orange; its complement is blue. Or take red-violet; its complement is yellow-green.

Complementary colors enhance and strengthen each other. When *red* is placed against a *green* background, it makes the *red* seem redder and the *green* more green. *Blue* does this to *orange, violet* affects *yellow* in this same fashion. Although this is of the most benefit to the scene designer it also applies to costuming. The effect of a green dress in a rose-walled room will be much more telling than if the walls had been painted aquamarine, for example.

Analogous colors are those we encounter as we go around the color wheel clockwise: the ones next to or related to each other. Going from noon to three, red, red-orange, orange, and yellow-orange are analogous colors. They go together, making a color harmony if they are the right shades of these colors. Used together their effect is more soothing, less disturbing, than the use of colors that complement each other. See how useful all this is? The audience at a play does not need to know color theory to be affected by it.

Consider the colors individually. We know both a little and quite a lot about them. Although color effect has only become a recognized part of mental therapy in the past few years, the great painters and writers such as Da Vinci and Goethe had already found out a great deal about its influence on people. Much of what they reported is still valid and some of their discoveries serve as a starting point today. (Cf. Birren, Faber, *Color*. The University Press, New Hyde Park, New York, 1963.)

Red is the color of joy, of sex, battle, activity, and of the extrovert. It is the warmest color and this applies to both meanings of the word warm. It is for the character that is outgoing, loving, or passionate. Usually it denotes a happy mood, but carried to the extremes it can also be the color for a manic mood. Remember that pink is a less flamboyant version of the same hue and that violet is red tempered with its opposite color, or nearly opposite, and see what character definition the costumer can create to help the playwright and the actor.

Blue is the color of the more introspective, inward-turned person. It denotes reflectivity, the working part of creativeness, intellectualism even. It is for the thoughtful, moody, or quiet soul. For most people it is a restful color, even inducing sleep, which makes it a fine shade to paint the bedrooms of insomniacs. If red is a happy color, blue is a sad one; most people who have a strong preference for blue tend to be pessimistic where a liking for red signifies an optimistic frame of mind. Tradition has made blue the color of virginity. Is it depressing to be a virgin?

Green is everybody's color, all things to all people . . . the great popular favorite. For this reason some people of an individualistic nature find it dull and uninteresting. It is the great middle-of-the-roader and remember most roads in nature are bordered with it. Nature has put more green in our lives than any other color and quite rightly. It is healing and soothing, a therapeutic color, and if we are blotting out the greens nature gave us with billboards and concrete roadways and buildings, we do it at our own risk. Green is not everybody's favorite color, it is too neutral—but it is the second choice of many. If you like green you are likely to be well-balanced, adaptable. It follows that you might be well liked yourself. If I were dressing a play involving presidential candidates I should dress the winning candidate in green— The People's Choice.

Yellow, the color of the sun's rays, is a rather infantile color. It is often a favorite with children or immature people. The child tends to prefer yellow, peach, or orange—and to discard these preferences as he grows up. It is not the color of an intellectual. I wouldn't dress a wise lady novelist in it, but it would be possible for the author of a cookbook.

These are the four main colors. Of the two remaining, purple has been demonstrated to be the least popular color, making it suitable for a villain to wear. Orange, though recently it has been given a high sanction by fashion, is the second least preferred. It is likely to be preferred by the lightweight, vacillating brain. Orange-lovers are often people whose opinions are easily swayed and whose friendships are not deep or lasting. But they do not like to be alone so they are constantly shifting social milieus.

There is another important category of color: the earth colors. Tan, brown, beige, gray, creamy neutrals, wood shades, and the brownish-brick hues. These are neutral, no-color colors. They represent withdrawal, evasion, treading water . . . background people, timid people, those who do not want to offend the powerful Red or come out positively in favor of the opposite Blue or Green. These are earth-color characters or the uncommitted person still emerging from the cocoon, whose color we do not know. As you can see, this is a large and very useful category in designing for Broadway.

This is only a once-over-lightly on an important subject. You can find out more by additional reading and you will undoubtedly make your own discoveries. One of the interesting facts is that the audience need not know any of this to respond to your use of it. A man will see red just as you want him to although he has never heard that red is an inflammatory color. The salesman from Dubuque in the fifth row

on the aisle will still think Miss Jane Jones the prettiest heroine who ever wore blue even if he doesn't know he is partial
to blue.

You can have your own version of Fun and Games with
this—Something to Think about while Waiting for a Bus.
Try dressing Ophelia. Should she begin in a radiant pink,
as the joyous love symbol, later having the pink overlaid with
gray-blue veils of a schizoid morbidity? Or should she wear
yellow and orange—that's for immaturity. Or try *Faust*. If
Mephistopheles were to wear red, a traditional devil color,
should Faust oppose him in green, his complementary color?
And should Marguerite be dressed in virginal blue?

Keeping in mind that the costumer must work with the
scene designer, the possibilities of what can be created with
color are both endless and challenging. Remember that the
hue of a color—one altered by the addition of another color,
such as making purple out of red by the addition of blue
—changes the significance of that color by having the same
affect that the added color has. On the other hand a tint,
which is what we get when we add white, such as turning red
into pink—represents the same emotional picture as the original primary color to a lesser degree. Aquamarine is still the
same green-blue as the peacock color from which it was
mixed, except that it is a younger preference. Gray is the
color, for instance, to depict wisdom and maturity, not simply what happens to our hair as we age. Generally the light
pastel shades are favored by the young. It is only as people
grow older that they tend to commit themselves to the
stronger, deeper colors. The very young do not see gray at
all. Black and white, though not actually colors, have come

through custom to represent certain things. White for inno-
cence, childhood—thence to childishness. Black is for mourning in most countries, or for the sedate, poised, even sophisticated. The woman who wants to remain an enigma should
wear black.

Real artists are usually by the very nature of their creative
ability perceptively in advance of the rest of mankind. In
relation to color both painters and writers have proved themselves avant-garde. This is also true, interestingly enough, of
songwriters. Take, for instance, the titles of these standards.
The men who originated these songs meant exactly what they
said, though there were no color analysts to advise them.
"Red Hot Mama" is about the kind of woman, sexy and
warm, who habitually prefers red. "Mood Indigo" is written
to be as blue as all get out. Or think of "Volare"—"Blue on
Blue." Take "Greensleeves"—remember how old it is—and
see if it isn't just the right song for that color. "Black Is the
Color of My True Love's Hair"—a dirge. And doesn't
everybody admire and dream of "Jeannie with the Light
Brown Hair"—a nice, neutral girl who is everybody's pinup.

Assume that the problem is the costuming of the heroine,
who may be a star, an ingenue, a leading woman, or a character actress. Heroines come in all shapes and sizes these days.
First, take into account her color preferences. If she has
said, "I simply loathe brown!" there is no point in trying to
change this loathing overnight—give in to it. After all there
are a lot of other colors no matter how chic you think it is
yourself. Or if she has said, "Any color as long as it is red!"
let her have it. Even if at first thought it doesn't seem to be

the perfect color, remember that with the blue-red range and the yellow-red range there must be at least a hundred shades of this one primary to choose from. Somewhere between pale tea rose and deep maroon there will be a color that will give you both what you want. So when your actress says that, don't just see red, think about it.

Now consider the character of the written part: what kind of heroine the woman is supposed to be. Is she gay and light-hearted or wistful and moody? Is she the queen of tragedy? As we know there are colors for all these characteristics.

If green is the voter's choice, he has his dislikes too. Last I checked, as mentioned before, purple was the least liked color. One wonders why kings wore "royal purple" unless they were just asking for trouble? Digging further into the records, however, we come up with the fact that the "royal purple" was pretty close to crimson, so perhaps the monarchy wasn't asking to be deposed after all.

Orange, as we've said, is the second least popular color, which may be why so many mothers have to be firm to get their offspring to drink their breakfast orange juice.

On the other hand, as with both orange juice and caviar, one must make allowances for acquired tastes. Staying with orange, a few years ago it was taken up enthusiastically as a new and not yet overdone color by the avant-garde interior decorators, textile designers, and couturiers. It became the rage and has persisted long enough to filter down to the lower-income brackets, who now accept it cheerfully, whereas a short time ago these same people would have said they hated orange. Remember, too, that basically your theatre audiences are among the most advanced groups. So with them it is likely that a basically unpopular color will change its status as soon as it becomes fashionable, as soon as everybody is wearing it or it is all over town. So if your play is a hit and runs for a year, better get a change of costume and color for that leading lady.

Time out for a digression. What about the supposed disadvantage of being bored with red hair and the poor boys who were called "Carrots" and hated it? Red hair isn't red; it's that color we were talking about, really. But when it became popular remember how many women started dyeing their hairdos that tangy color?

Since black, aside from being the obvious color for sophistication, is also the traditional color for mourning, Hamlet is correctly dressed—"'Tis not alone my inky cloak, good mother, nor customary suits of solemn black, nor windy suspiration of forced breath . . ." But that is only from here to Denmark. In Japan, for instance, white is the color for mourning. The deceased is still often dressed in white and it is the color of the paper flower wreaths and the long poles that support them in funeral processions. But until we decide this East-West controversy, white is certainly the color for peace, contentment, and—youthful purity.

Brown, taupe, gray, and beige are the neutrals. They have definite uses as a suspension of color, a rest period. They can also reflect hesitation, lack of decision, a refusal to take sides. And they are, unfortunately, almost the entire color range in a man's modern wardrobe. I do not wish to suggest that abstinence from positive color keeps man uncommitted.

These are rather strong statements about the meanings of these various hues and there will be people who will disagree with them. You may ask if there also will not be hundreds of ticket purchasers in the audiences who will not know or care about color? So why bother? Because in this area it is not what people know that counts, but how they feel, react. Whether they realize that they are made happier by a good big slug of bright red doesn't matter. What does count is that you can, to a certain extent at least, increase their euphoria to a higher level without their knowing it—or lower it if that is the intention of the play. The fascinating thing is that *it can be done by color.*

The lighting expert knows this, of course, and perhaps uses this factor even more consciously than anyone else in the theatre. As discussed earlier, he really subjects the subconsciousness of the audience to manipulation by gelatins, pinks and amber, blue and green.

There is a very old Chinese game in which a piece of paper is cut into seven segments of specified but assorted shapes and sizes. The expert at this game is able to create from this small handful of pictures of anything he chooses—a bird, a horse, a monastery on a hill—by skillful placement. The amount we don't know about color psychology often makes us feel like the beginner at the Chinese puzzle game; but there is, when one starts work at fitting the few bits and pieces together, a surprising amount to be done.

Let's pick a heroine and see what we can do for her with color before we shop for or design the particular dresses she will wear. We can't use Eleanor Roosevelt in *Sunrise At Campobello,* though there is a build to the play that would respond to this treatment. Any actual historical character so partial to a particular color that it is known as Eleanor Blue during her lifetime will have to be approached from some other angle. Neither is *Two for the Seesaw* a good practice play for this chapter—Gittel Mosca was a creature of such varying moods that her colors were kaleidoscopic. She wore pink, red, black, blue, green, and yellow, with a couple of stripes and plaids thrown in to keep it lively. With luck the audience never noticed all this, only Anne Bancroft herself.

For reasons like the ones above, as you can see, it is very difficult to pick cases to use as examples. Also we want characters who are reasonably well known to us all. Let us try three fairly classic heroines—beginning with Lady Macbeth in the tragedy. Or Liza Doolittle in *Pygmalion*. Or Mrs. Antrobus in Thornton Wilder's *The Skin of Our Teeth*. Take whichever of these three you prefer and plot out a color scheme for her wardrobe with no relation of course to the scenic background, specified season of the year, or fashion. Those are factors that are considered later in a different context. If you want to give yourself an added handicap, pretend that your unknown heroine has a color allergy or two or some violent preference. Then, using what we have just sketched in as to the whims and humors of the various hues, make yourself a color diagram for the play.

You can make this as simple or as difficult as you wish. To complicate it further remember that the other characters' costumes will impinge on this one woman's wardrobe and you can keep the *emotional* effect of this in mind. For instance, recollect the scene in *Pygmalion* where Eliza is brought home from the ball by two men who will be wearing formal evening clothes of black and white? The housekeeper comes into that scene, too. What will this do to the balance of color power?

When you have finished, try to give yourself reasons for everything you did. Why is this woman "in the pink" or that one "blue as all get out"? Perhaps you will find that you chose certain things instinctively, as you thought, but when you come to analyze them, there were sound basic reasons for your decisions.

If you score yourself fairly high on this first run-through, here is a tougher one. Suppose that the actress playing the part will not wear any shade of yellow—from the palest creamy beige to a deep custardy brown. Now dress the heroine in *Who's Afraid of Virginia Woolf?*

12

High Style — Low Fashion

Whether we intend it to or not, fashion has always played a large part in theatrical production. Sometimes its influence is completely unintentional. It is simply that our eyes have become so accustomed to its dictates that we accept them, or achieve them, without in the least realizing that we are doing so.

Examine the portraits of any of the famous actresses of the last century—Duse, Bernhardt, Mrs. Siddons. Most of the extant pictures of these great ladies will be in full rig for one of their great parts. Portia, Ophelia, Lady Macbeth, etc. They may have thought they were dressed according to the period they were playing, and so may the designers who created their clothes for them. But after studying their costumes, turn to the clothes for the period in which they were performing, and look at the influence of current fashion on the young lady of Denmark, for instance. Something rotten here, too. Now think back about your own designing for a period piece. In an era of narrow skirts or dropped waistlines, haven't you tended to narrow the skirts and drop the waistlines of a moyen-âge lady? Don't we all tend to put Mary, Queen of Scots, in a shift?

No matter how pure we try to keep our designing eye, we cannot help but be affected by the constant bombardment of what we see in store windows, restaurants, and the fashion magazines. Sometimes we learn to like things that, in our first reaction, we knew were bad for the human figure from the principle of pure design. Conversely, if a great French couturier or a beautifully shaped Hollywood star came out with an endorsement of clothes whose fullness started right below the bust, our own designs for a show laid in the Middle Ages are more apt to incorporate unashamedly that pregnant fullness. I once managed to reconcile an actress to the clothes she would have to wear in a play set in the middle twenties by showing her, line for line, exactly where those clothes duplicated some of the fashions we were wearing that year. Then she decided she would not look silly or frumpy. On the other hand, remember the flapper clothes of the twenties that made us all laugh heartily when we saw old snapshots of them in the forties and fifties? Laugh at them we might, but ten years later every woman on the street had squeezed her unsuitable figure into a short-skirted shift as close to the John Held tradition as she could afford.

It is this kind of trickiness on the part of Dame Fashion that should make us watch our steps. Particularly when you couple this with the fact that there are certain elements stage clothing has to have, fashionable or not.

What are these required elements? Movement is one. The

ability to move, freely and easily for the actress, the appearance of movement from the audience's point of view. The actress must never look as if she is straining herself or her seams to get around the stage. She must never appear to have sat so long on that couch because her skirt was too tight for her to get up. If the skirt is too tight, it will be full of distasteful wrinkles when she does rise, and she may have to spend precious stage moments rearranging her clothing that will seem to distort her character portrayal. Or she may have had to sit there pulling that hem down over her knees to the fidgeting discomfort of both herself and the people watching her. A bad bit of business for a modest woman playing a suave and sophisticated part.

On the other hand, style should be one of the major components of theatrical clothes. Sometimes the style is attributable to the actress herself, or to the actor. The greatest exponent of style I know of is Miss Lynn Fontanne. Anyone who saw Miss Fontanne in *The Visit* will remember what I am talking about. I do not mean that the clothes she wore were unfashionable. It is simply that the really plus quality those costumes had came from inside the star herself.

What do the two words—style and fashion—mean here? The dictionary offers us a variety of meanings that is bewildering but for the purposes of this discussion, I boil it down to this:

Fashion: The prevailing mode.

Style: An individual expression . . . in relation to the arts.

Given those two distinctions, which would you choose? It is not a bad question, since it is a choice the designer is often called upon to make.

Certain plays automatically relieve the designer of the necessity for making this choice. Take such plays as *Sabrina Fair, Kind Sir, The Pleasure of His Company.* In these a need for a fashionable type of dressing is part of the script. Clothing here serves not only as a status symbol that helps the audience place the characters as soon as the curtain rises, it also helps reflect an inner status that lies in the minds of the characters. On the other hand, some plays, such as Tennessee Williams' *Summer and Smoke* or *The Glass Menagerie,* demand unfashionable clothing—without shifting into the realm of "costume" dramas. The unworldliness of the clothing here depicts the divorce from reality of the Williams women. To swing to the other extreme, a play such as *The Madwoman of Chaillot,* though it has some of the aspects of a costume piece, makes a positive demand for style, particularly in the apparel of the four female cronies.

Go over in your mind the requirements of good stage clothing. Movement we have already mentioned. Remember this means not only the fluidity of the clothing itself but the ability of the body to articulate itself within the cage of clothes. Any member of Actors' Equity can tell you that acting is done with the body as well as with the voice. Examine what these professionals wear to rehearse in, and you will find that they all prefer things that provide the maximum amount of freedom, no matter how unfashionable it makes them appear for the time being.

Grace is another important characteristic, for men as well as women. Some actors are so little endowed with this quality that they must depend on the designer to provide or enhance it for them. Sometimes, as with a horse, it depends on proper shoeing. Both slue-footedness and a tendency toward the pigeon-toed can be improved by the correct weighting on a shoe—a function more accurately performed by a podiatrist than by Ferragamo. Suppose the problem is knees that knock. This is hardly going to be solved by tight skirts that end somewhere about two inches above the point of conjuncture, is it?

Another thing—the clothes must always seem to belong to the actor—be his very own. Onstage they are part and parcel of his identity, who he is supposed to be. To make the leap from the actual card-carrying member of Equity, George Spelvin, to the romantic hero of *Gunsmoke* or *Julius Caesar* is often difficult enough, and the last thing the actor needs is to be hampered by his clothing. The clothing, modern dress or costume, should take the first step for him into the land of make-believe—a step so sure that the make-believe is lost in belief.

Every designer, after he has been working awhile, will develop his own list of theatrical requirements for costume. You may have several of your own as you read this. For me, one of the prime characteristics has always been that clothes should add beauty in the eye of the beholder. As a great millinery creator, Sally Victor, once said, if a hat doesn't make you look prettier than you are, don't buy it. The public who attend plays, movies, operas, and concerts want its stars to be beautiful or handsome. Even the villains of the piece must have the beauty of being thoroughly villainous. For this reason the good designer needs to learn what things will do most to cover the flaws and uncover the best features. One of the best assets any of us possesses is the human body.

This is not intended as an advocacy of the topless bathing suit or evening gown, but, rather, for clothes that conform to, or parallel the human figure, male or female. Men should look like men, and women should not. Shoulders should look like shoulders, waists like waists, not hips, breasts like breasts, etc. This does not mean that clothes on stage should be as revealing as an Elizabethan codpiece. There are ways of displaying sexuality that do not involve exposing it and stripping off all the glamour. But if a belt is worn at the waistline, accentuating the curve above and the swell below, instead of riding precariously on a hipbone where it will not stay unless anchored down, what have we lost? Only a basically ludicrous effect. By and large the most becoming clothes are the ones that conform to or go along with what the figure does, not fight against it. For an example, look at the pages on "Frontier Clothes" in *What People Wore*.

Now back to style versus fashion. How many of the few things named here as necessary to theatrical clothing are inherent in the fashion of this exact moment? In the past ten years of fashion history, has there been one year that would permit you to fill those requirements fashionably? Only by compromise, which is, I suppose, one of the things you must learn to do, if you are not going to compromise with principle. Oh, feet of clay!

Even fashionable fabrics can work against you. Can you remember that period in the 1950s when there was a mad vogue for the very stiff, elaborate, heavy—and how heavy! —silks of the Orient for cocktail dresses, theatre coats, and formal suits? Most women waiting to be taken out after five o'clock had to wait standing, probably praying for a Hollywood reclining board to lean back on. Once you sat down in those gorgeous garments you were undone, certainly from the rear view, and often with nasty and ineradicable creases across the front as well. Unless you stood up for the entire party, it was best to make your exits as if from the presence of royalty, backing out. What price fashion?

If it were necessary, which thank God it is not, to confine oneself to one fabric in which to costume an entire play, which would serve the purpose best? I have thought about it a good deal, and my vote would go, I believe, to wool jersey, if all weights could be included. If I could have just three fabrics on stage, I would take jersey, chiffon, and either a fine Pima cotton if the play were modern, or cotton velveteen, if it were a period piece. What is the use of this kind of conjecture? Simply to tell you what materials are the most satisfactory. If you have two dresses to choose from, select the one made of chiffon, not of taffeta, all other things being equal.

One other personal preference. You may skip these sections on the soapbox if you wish. There is a definite value, in my opinion, to the natural fibers, silk, wool, cotton, and even linen. You can tell how they will behave, and they certainly have it all over the synthetics in the matter of "hand," which *shows* from the audience's point of view.

Crazes for certain colors are another of fashion's foibles. We have already discussed color onstage in another chapter. To go into the spectrum again would be repetitious, except to say that fashionable coloring should be used in costuming, like any other of fashion's weapons, to score a point when it will serve to do so. When you wish to present a woman who is dedicated to things à la mode, by all means have her wear the most à la mode color, *if* that color does not conflict with some other factor, such as scenery, that has to be considered.

Perhaps the above dissatisfaction with the fashion scene on the stage comes from the fact that we have been going through a long dry spell. For more years than it is cheering to count, the *Vogue's* Eye View has been one unusually unadaptable to the theatre. It is easy enough to look back, after the mode is a thing of the past and evaluate its stage presence. While we are living in it, and wearing it, it is much harder to make decisions about its essential worthiness based on a sound value judgment.

One of the last periods of really lovely clothes for stage purposes that I remember are the ones my own mother wore at the end of World War I. I have recollections of beautiful gracious, flowing garments swirling around a very beautiful woman. Perhaps this is all wrong. Perhaps it is just simply that I loved my mother.

Make this test for yourself: Go over the fashions of the last fifty years. There are not too many books on the subject, it is too new. The best I know of are the English works of a woman, Grace Langley-Moore, who has specialized in the more recent period. Her books are amusing, as she photographs the actual costumes, sometimes with famous actresses such as Beatrice Lillie or Margot Fonteyn, wearing the clothes. If you cannot get her books, the best source for this period is to study the magazines. *Vogue* is fine, if you can locate a complete collection. Other good sources are the pattern mag-

azines, such as *Butterick* or *McCalls*. Now, going through
them from fashion upheaval to major earthquake, look for the
years in which the clothes of the prevailing mode would have
made good theatrical clothing. Don't place any bets on the
outcome, unless you are ready to bet against fashion. And if
you can lay hands on the old pattern books, and get the same
ones I found in our attic, don't think that 1966 is so avant-
garde. The ones I saw had the models wearing light green
and mauve hair. Another good resource for this period is old
photograph and snapshot albums, if you can get hold of a full
collection.

Skipping hastily over the sections on Mother Love and
green or purple hair, go through these looking at the clothes,
not Aunt Bessie's avoirdupois. Make your own evaluation of
how these clothes would conform to stage requirements. How
many years out of the fifty-odd are fashion and theatre com-
patible? Very few, I am afraid. But if you can compare
these pictures with, say, Daniel Blum's photographic histories
of Broadway, you can find, among the funny clothes, many
photographs that have both style and distinction.

When these two qualities are both there, it is usually a
happy marriage between the player and the designer. They
need each other's best qualities to bring it off. I remember
a play called *Amphitrion 38,* designed by Valentina, performed by the Lunts. It was, in that era, a joy to the eye
as well as the ear. Valentina was a Russian woman who
designed perfectly beautiful clothes that were never in fashion,
always had great style. Only the most knowing and educated
clothes observer even thought of trying to copy one of her

tours de force. She designed only for the very rich and let the poor go.

I was costumed by Valentina just once, while I was doing that part of my apprenticeship in the theatre called being an actress. It was a play called *Come of Age,* with Judith Anderson as the star, and I was being paid the magnificent sum of thirty-five dollars a week, on which I had to live. During the period of being fitted for that brown tulle cocktail party dress, which was certainly the most gorgeous garment I had owned—no, worn—up to that point in my life, the producer's wife decided that Valentina clothes were perfect for me. "Why don't you talk to her? I'm sure she will make some arrangement so that you can pay her off in installments?"

Valentina's dresses began at about two-fifty and soared rapidly, a lot of money for the early thirties, and on thirty-five a week. But I would have loved to wear them, so I was brave and asked. Madame V was most gracious. She thought about my problem and then suggested a floor-length gray wool, a sort of monk's robe type, for me to wear in the daytime. For evening I could have the exact same garment in black velvet. It was the same dress she was making for Gladys Swarthout and the producer's wife that season. They often met socially, but the duplication didn't seem to bother either of them. I never fraternized in such circles, but it bothered me.

Further, I was to discard all my garments of heterogeneous origin, throw away all my coats, and settle for one to be worn everywhere. This was to be a floor-length cape of brown beaver, very, very chic. The approximate cost, oh, maybe nine hundred dollars. I didn't earn that much a year in the theatre, that year . . .

Well, thinking it over, I decided not to be dressed by Madame Valentina. The producer's wife was driven to rehearsals in a Rolls-Royce. I went in a subway, unless I was saving money and walking. I simply could not bear my foreseeable damage to the great clothes. On the subway, all those floor-length models could get so terribly dirty at the hems.

This chapter has been included more to set the reader thinking than to set down any hard and fast rules. The subjects discussed are too much a matter of taste for them to have fostered any rigid regulations. For the final question, what garment has, more than any other, all the basic elements of style inherent in it? To me, without a quibble, it is the cape. Rarely really fashionable, it has been worn longer than skirts or, that comparative newcomer, trousers. Look at some of the old cave paintings, and what is that old lion skin around the figure's neck but the ancestor of a gendarme's outfit? Worn by both men and women, long or short, it is the apparel of gods and goddesses, heroes or Svengalis. Bullfighters or early Christians, Romans or wistful little women, female Civil War spies or modern Marine Corps officers, French schoolgirls or the actors of the Old Vic, all have gained luster and stature from its graceful and effective envelopment. It may not, at this precise moment, be the height of fashion, but it can surely mold a form with style. When in doubt, try a cape as a little something to wrap around that heroine before the landlord throws her out into the storm.

13

The Reflecting Eye

No management expects the costume designer to perform a miracle with the actors' appearance—a near miracle will do nicely, thank you.

The costume designer is not required to be an expert on fashionable hair styling or a makeup artist, but it is certainly assumed that he will be. So under the circumstances, it is just as well to arm yourself with a few bits of information and hope that with clear sailing and the wind at your back you can muddle through.

During this era of the theatre, the tendency has been to reduce makeup for men to a minimum, except for an occasional enhancement of eyes, definition of lips, or the blocking out of a bad defect. So let us consider makeup from the feminine point of view, remembering that everything we learn in an actress's dressing room can be applied to actors, since Boul Armenia is fortunately bisexual.

If you haven't done this already, pick the most experienced actress you know and arrange to pay a call on her in her dressing room at the theatre just as she is ready to put on her makeup. By most experienced I mean the one who will have applied theatrical makeup the most times. Pay for your visit with charming conversation, a brand-new joke, or a bunch of rambler roses, but tell her why you are there. Get her to explain what she is doing while she is doing it. See how carefully she cleans her face so as to start with basic essentials. Watch the various shades that probably go into her foundation color. Very few people use it just as it comes from the tube or pot. When she begins blocking, as she probably will, see how and ask why.

Most good makeup artists begin with the eyes, after the foundation is on. There is a good reason for this. Eyes are an actor's most effective feature, and if you put on the lipstick before the eye masking, you may be distracted by all that bright red so that you neglect eyes and brows. These latter should be enhanced enough to carry the face if the performer had to go on suddenly without completing the job. Note that little daub of paste rouge or lipstick that goes in the inner angle of the eye. That touch of red serves two purposes. It stops the eye from out front, gives it definition; and the red contrast whitens the white of the eye itself, makes it look clearer and more luminous. The penciled outlines on the upper and lower lids also "stop" the eye, so they must be far enough apart to be sure the eye appears large enough. Some actresses have abandoned those penciled lines, feeling that the cosmetic or mascara on the lashes does this effectively enough. Since street makeup has become so elaborate and has all that Italian exaggeration, it is sometimes hard to tell whether a woman is in full Broadway war paint, or just done up for luncheon at a chic restaurant, and actually a very few more additions would enable most of us to go from lunch right onstage.

If your actress blocks her face, straightening a beaked or retroussée nose or taking some of the sag out of heavy jowls, this is fascinating to watch. It is usually done with white grease, and straight lines on each side of the nose, but must be seen to be understood properly.

Usually the last part of the face to be made up is the mouth. If a heavy enough base foundation has been used, the entire original outline of the lips can be obliterated, and a new mouth drawn in, of any shape desired. This, tight-lipped, cold, or full, generous, and sensual, or anything in between. Most actresses are not willing to change their lips enough, they have become so accustomed to them. Often they need, for stage purposes, to be made larger. Generally, as people grow older, their lips appear to shrink, unnoticed by them, and this must be compensated for. Watch what the color of the lipstick used does for the color of the teeth. To whiten the appearance of the teeth, a true rosy red is effective with most people. It can be as salutary, in effect, as a trip to the dentist for a cleaning.

There are all kinds of extra added attractions that can be done in the makeup area, but these are the province of the professional makeup expert. Simple things such as false eyelashes you know about; these are often so successful onstage they may be called a fringe benefit of Actors' Equity. There is also the possibility of making one eye appear to diverge from the other by a difference in the makeup of the two.

There is putty to build up or indicate a broken nose. For the part of Captain Hook or one of the Pirates of Penzance, a tooth can appear to be missing from a few yards away if it is simply blacked out—covered with black eyebrow pencil. And for special effect, there are such things as the two pieces of apple Helen Hayes is supposed to have worn in her cheeks in *Victoria Regina*. Things like this are simply the tricks of the trade.

The costume designer may be asked, usually by the performer himself, to look out for something on the night of dress rehearsal. You may wish you had four pair of eyes by the time you have watched for troubles in your own territory, plus checking the makeup foundation color of one, the effect of the lighting on the eye shade of another. If there are serious flaws, the management needs to hire a makeup specialist. Some managements automatically do this anyway, particularly in costume plays, and if it can be afforded, it is well worth the expenditure.

Hair styling is a more simple problem of design, and therefore more naturally in the costumer's province. You do not need to be a hairdo specialist with an exact knowledge of the reverse curl or teasing. A rudimentary appraisal of the current hair styles will do you. Aside from that, what you need is your own design ability, with special attention to line and balance. Consider the relation of the size of the head to the body, when viewed from a distance. Should the hair be thicker, more fluffed out, to make the head seem larger? Many people seem to dwindle away at the top, rise to a pinpoint. Or should the hair be cut shorter or thinned, to avoid the lion-headed look?

Then consider the hair in relation to the face. Does the hair style minimize the face, make the features appear too small by contrast? Should the lines of the hairdo go up, to lift and brighten an otherwise sagging physiognomy? Or should the lines run down to lengthen a moonface? Should the curls be spread at eye level to help widen the face at this point, or do you need height on top to shape the head as a whole properly? This is the kind of thing to look for and make recommendations on. Then tell it to the actress so she may tell her hairdresser.

It is sometimes a good idea to get started early in this area. If you are dealing with someone who appears to have poor judgment in this respect, who turns up daily with the hair "badly designed," suggest an early trip to the hairdresser to have the hair set the way she plans to wear it in the play. This gives you all the time you will need to rectify the seasoning without having to plunge in so abruptly that you hurt feelings. "Your hair curls so naturally, why not try pulling a few curls out around your temples?" Besides, it may take more than one trip to the beauty parlor to accomplish what you have in mind.

If the problem is color, you need all the time you can get. Suppose the hair has to be dyed or bleached. None of the extreme changes ever come out exactly right the first time. You may have a lady with pink hair instead of blond, or purple instead of black the first time she tries. And if you start having real color problems, remember a wig covers a multitude of sins.

It is not only in *Life with Father* that you have a coloring problem. You need balance and variety in hair shades as well as in the clothes. Or the words "brassy blonde" may appear in the author's description, and the casting has been done with a fine actress whose hair is mouse-colored. Or you may need to make the boy and girl who play brother and sister look more alike by matching their hair shades. One thing: If the actress has to dye her hair or change it radically to conform with the script or to avoid conflict with another actress, find out if management has agreed to pay for this. Sometimes it is in the contract, and since it is often very expensive to go from dark to bright, it is advisable to know who picks up the tab. By and large, the best hairdressing comes high. Suspect a bargain price here, unless it is for program credit.

In spite of their recent fashion prevalence, I am against wigs. Where they are a necessity, such as to cover a bald spot or to hide a receding hairline with "hair-laces," use them if you must. "Falls"—those tails of hair that get combed in with the actress's own to add length or abundance—are not bad, since most women can cope successfully with these. The same is certainly true of simple chignon. But beware of the full headpiece, much as your actress may urge for one at the beginning.

At that beginning, they are violently expensive. Then, they are never right or comfortable the first time around. They are murder under a hat, and pervert the hat to be worn. Since they need as constant fixing as real hair on the head, they are always at a beauty parlor being dressed, and soon you will have a request for two, one for at the salon, one for the theatre, at five hundred dollars or better per skullcap. And last, after the show has been running a very few weeks, you will find the actress going on *au naturel,* while her wig remains on a stand in her dressing room. "Nothing," she will tell you cheerfully, "like having worn a wig for a few weeks to make you appreciate the joys of your own hair."

You may find that these peripheral portions of the designing business include everything from the tactful suggestion that she use phony fingernails to a nail-biting, hypertense female, to the suggestion of elevator shoes to a too-short juvenile, via a coeducational lecture on a good deodorant to anyone in the cast. Take these duties in stride, they are all part of the job. But in the last week or so you have a special function in relation to the people for whom you have designed a wardrobe. You must serve as the mirror in which they can really see all of themselves.

The mirror on the wall of their dressing table is too small, it is only two-dimensional. They cannot tell how they are projected to the balcony, unless you will climb all the way up there and give a look. They need to know what lighting, not the circle of bulbs around a makeup mirror, but stage spots and footlights, do to their face, figure, and skin. They need to know how they look from the rear, side, and front, sitting down, in motion, the physical effectiveness of an entrance or exit. Are they standing up straight enough? Are they walking slue-footed or pigeon-toed? Most important of all, how do they look in relation to the other people with whom they appear on-stage? The director can tell them how they *act,* but you are the one who can tell how they look, and if there is trouble, give constructive advice.

Don't rush in where no angel would be caught soiling his golden slippers, and leave well enough alone, for God's sake.

But when asked, give helpful and constructive advice, or keep your mouth shut. Don't ever hurt an actor where he is most vulnerable, in his ego, just before the opening. Be sure you can put the pieces together again before you take them apart. Never start a sentence, "I don't know just what's wrong, but there's something funny looking about your . . ." In the confines of your area, you are jolly well supposed to know what's wrong, and how to fix it. As a mirror, try to reflect as truly and clearly as you can. Broadway is no carnival, though it may seem so at times. And as a reflector, you must never be one of the distorting mirrors of a fun house.

An actress friend of mine, who is a leading lady both on-stage and in television, has just finished reading the manuscript of this chapter. All through the section on wigs she emitted clucking sounds of disapproval. Since I am all in favor of granting equal time to both sides, I feel that I should add here at least the gist of what she said.

"Not snow, nor rain, nor dark of night—nor a weekend in the sun and surf of Fire Island—" is what it boils down to. If you wear a wig in a play, you can always go on, no matter what the weather outside or your private life may have been. It must be admitted that that is reassuring, and for the actress without digital dexterity in the matter of hair styling, it could be a lifesaver. It is also a time-saver, since clapping a wig over your own out-of-order hairdo is a lot quicker than the time that must be given to rollers and re-setting on one of the bad days. There!

Scrambling back to my own side of the fence, I hasten to point out that the last few shows in which this actress appeared on Broadway were either musicals, or period pieces with such extravagant productions that they were done on the scale of musicals without the music. In productions of this caliber a certain exaggeration of both makeup and hair styling is desirable, and there are both hairdressers and makeup experts always in the theatre to lend a hand with the resetting of that wig, and its putting on. These wigs were used to create character effects that would not have been possible with the actress's own hair.

Final rebuttal: This same leading lady recently bought herself a very expensive wig for her private life. It was constantly at the makers for redoing, and after about six months she gave it to her best friend. It came back to her, after the friend had tried it for a while and decided she would rather be poorly coiffed.

14

What if You Can't Draw a Straight Line?

One of the real problems for any designer, custom or theatrical, is how to display what he is selling. The custom designer has this advantage—he can, if he can afford the great expense, make up a collection of models, which he can show on mannequins, and then take orders on them. For obvious reasons, this will not work in the theatre. Models for the costumes of *Carmen Jones* are not likely to attract a producer of *The Subject Was Roses*. But the resourceful costumer does have three or four ways of coping with the situation.

The most common and accepted way is to show sketches. If you can draw, fine, and here is another chapter you can ignore. But I have never been able to draw, which I insist did not diminish my ability to design. I worked in the fabric itself, which gave me an exact feeling for the dress. Working with a dressmaker dummy, and yards of unbleached muslin, I made what was the first pattern for the dress. But this is hardly practical as a thing on which to get that OK from the producer that is so essential. Neither does it enchant most actresses who are more literal and need to see more exactly what the dress will look like. And it is certainly no way to cinch that job you haven't got yet.

First let me make the suggestion that you may not be as bad at sketching as you think. Fashion sketches should be in a loose, free style. Academic figure drawing would actually inhibit the appearance of the presentation. You do not want to be Michelangelo; Toulouse-Lautrec made much better fashion sketches. So avoid anything that tightens up your drawing. This was one of the reasons I knew my own sketches were bad. The further away from childhood I got, the more constipated my work appeared. But where after four years of graphic art at college and another ten of trying to apply what I had been taught I knew I made bad sketches, my seven-year-old daughter came up a dozen times in her untutored way with a crayon something that had ten times the charm and dash I was laboring so hard to achieve.

The good art schools all over the country recognize that fashion drawing is a technique by itself, and will try to help you evolve a stylized system of your own. You do not have to draw perfect hands and feet, remember. You do not really have to draw a figure at all, if you can think of an alternate hanger to put clothes on, perhaps even some way of rendering a simple hanger.

Or suppose that while you can't draw, you can paint. Try working right in watercolor or tempora. Or can you draw in crayon better than in pencil? Then use crayon, or pastels, or even charcoal, with perhaps a half-inch line of watercolor wash to indicate the shade you are also presenting with your attached swatches.

I once saw some enchanting designs that were like a collage, made of thin, shiny, accurately colored paper put together in blocks, in the proper proportions. Say, for instance, on gray charcoal paper there was a white rectangle, proper size for a blouse, pasted above a dark green rectangle, slightly larger, for the skirt. Then a very stylized figure from a pattern throwaway booklet had been traced on over this in the proper place, using brown carbon paper. Paint on long eyelashes in color, and you have a sensation—if the design is a good one.

There are all kinds of ways of faking sketches. I know one man who works in makeup, eye shadow, mascara, lipstick, and rouge, and who gets a very professional effect from this. I know another who makes a rather too tight rendering in watercolor and then frees the whole thing by a not too wet wash over it all in some pale shade when it is completed. There is also the device of getting an accomplished artist to make you three or four or five figures that you can use to trace over, and then, working with good architectural tracing paper, ink or pencil in an outline, or color right over them. If you have a wide enough selection, no one need ever know what you have been up to.

With a wide enough variety of paints and papers to fool around with, you can make a nice mess and take up quite a lot of time. But if after all this turns out to be more fun than functional, and you are not satisfied with any of the results, there is still one last desperate step you can take. You can hire yourself a professional sketcher.

Even though we cannot do a thing well ourselves, we are still apt to be very fussy about the skills of someone else doing it for us, particularly when it is going out over our own signatures. While it may be hard to find the right sketcher, there are quite a few places in which to look. Basically, the quest is for a commercial artist with fashion experience. Some of these advertise in the Situations Wanted columns of the daily papers, and that is a fairly good place to begin. You never can tell until you have seen samples of work done by the artist, so if a phone conversation sounds reasonably hopeful, you must arrange an interview. If the sketches are good, before you close the deal, ask the man or woman to make a sketch for you there on the spot. This may make the applicant nervous, but you need to find out how fast he can work. The exigencies of the theatre being what they are, you just might need a dozen or more sketches done overnight.

Another place where good sketchers congregate is around the pattern companies, Vogue, Simplicity, Advance, etc. Some of them are agreeable about having their artists do outside work, and you can just call the Personnel Department and ask. People in this line of work almost always seem to be in need of extra money, and it is a shame not to give them the opportunity to earn it.

If you live in a city that carries *Women's Wear Daily* on its stands, this is another good Situations Wanted column to watch. Sketchers who want work in the wholesale areas this paper caters to are apt to have more dash and flair and be more exactly pointed in the right direction for the costume designer's purposes than those who work for the more stodgy pattern companies.

Another place to explore is the fashion trade schools. Or colleges that have good graphic arts departments. Or you might have a friend at the union who will fill in for you here, although, if you think about it, this is sometimes a rather risky proposition. . . .

Anyway, gold is where you find it, so keep your eyes open and let your need be known. You never can tell when someone will call you and say, "Are you still looking for a person to do sketches for you?" It might be your photographer friend who has a retoucher who can draw like a dream. In that case, you can be sure the eyelashes will be done with artistry. I once had sketches made for me by Lisette, the lovely young wife of Hilaire Hilar, author of *From Nudity to Raiment.* Her distinguished husband didn't mind her doing this kind of hackwork, since she was out apprenticing in order to learn the dress business, and I had a year or so more experience than she. And the best artist I ever had was a nurse who had been to Traphagen, when I could catch him between cases. What you will have to pay for these art forms must be open to negotiation. There is no "going rate." After all, how much is a picture?

The time may come when you and some management will know each other well enough so that you will not have to submit sketches. You may just be able to talk a dress, or a whole show. But this takes a certain kind of genius, too. Don't count on its happening to you very soon. Of course, if drawing is a problem, you may want to concentrate on found shows instead of designed ones. This is a good and necessary part of the profession. But you will have to abandon, for instance, all thought of doing a musical. More and more musicals are the center of the money machine. They are also one of the best ways to enhance your reputation and get you the big offers to do such films as *Cleopatra*. And instead of going to Spain, Italy, or England you might just have to spend that long hot summer at home.

In case you should have qualms about using someone else's talent with the pen, it is unnecessary. The practice is quite widespread although I must admit that I have encountered ghost-drawing more in Hollywood than in the East. This is possibly because it is easier to pay for out there, via the studio. I have one friend who worked her way all the way up to an Oscar by doing the art work for a head of wardrobe department who never gave her credit until, at the end, when she threatened to leave, he had to. This is one thing you can do, give credit. You can even let your sketcher sign his drawings.

One of the most famous of Hollywood designers was Irene, who was the star performer of Bullocks' custom-made department as well as one of the great favorites of the many stars she dressed. Certainly this woman was a success, and yet she hired sketchers. I am quite sure of this because when I was once interviewed by her as a possible "assistant," I did not qualify because I couldn't draw, although Lord knows I could do everything else that would have marked me as a good assistant, including make the dress, if I had to. And I saw a couple of sketchers busily at work in her studio while I was there, with no attempt at secrecy. I must say that Irene, who was called simply that, in the same way that one name was enough to designate the luminosity of Garbo, was very charming in her manner of turning down a candidate for the job.

On the other hand, there is Dorothy Jeakins, who is one of the most talented and successful designers we have today. If you can ever get your hands on a Jeakins drawing, make off with it. They are little works of art. Quite unlike what you would expect as a fashion sketch, they look like real people wearing real clothes. The drawing for the bonnets for *Friendly Persuasion* that I saw at Western Costume, where they were being executed, looked like sketches made on a Quaker street during the 1860s, rather than something conjured up over a studio drawing board. I am sure that her craftsmanship with the pencil must have been a great asset in getting started in her profession.

What I am trying to boil it down to is this: Anxious though you might be to get out and get on with the work, don't rush yourself into the river of competition and bypass that drawing lesson. If you think that you can learn to draw, take the time for it. As Richard Rodgers advises—and there's a man who certainly knows what he's talking about—"Stay in school."

15

The Tricks of the Trade

Full of that sublime self-confidence that comes of considering one's self a young genius, with the hearty backing of close friends and relatives, it came as a shock to realize that there were things I didn't understand about my chosen field. The first example of this I can remember came on the day Dorothy Fox, the dancer, spoke casually of the fact that a certain dance costume needed to be a breakaway. I was expected to start whipping one up immediately, and I didn't even know what one looked like.

By asking around I found out, of course, and one of the things I found out was that of all things, it is not supposed to look like itself. In other words, this kind of costume must not telegraph ahead the fact that it is going to break away—come off quickly. It is used when a supersonic costume change must be made, sometimes in front of the audience, which means it also has to be done gracefully. If the change is done backstage, the motions involved in making it need not remind one of Tallchief dancing in *Aurora's Wedding,* and the actor can employ the assistance of a dresser. Basically, however, there just aren't that many varieties of quick-change costumes.

The first one I made is pretty standard. In street clothing, the coatdress comes as close as anything. Substitute a full-length zipper for that row of buttons down the front, and you nearly have it. Or use the very large size snaps that can be pulled apart with one simple twist of the wrist for the whole line of fastenings, and you come closer to what I did. Then move this line of snaps off dead center to run from shoulder, to underarm to hem, as not being so obvious an eye-catcher, and there you are. As a rule, it doesn't matter how long it takes to get into the thing. It's the getting out of it that counts. The objection to the zipper is that it only runs in a straight line and will not curve around an armseye, so there is still the problem of opening up the neckline of a side closure. Now that the separating fasteners have become longer and more available, it is an excellent device whenever the opening run is a straight one, and there is time, when dressing, to fiddle with the insertion of the tiny free end of the fastener and get it in the little groove. Otherwise stick to the huge snaps. But if you are using these, be sure the balance of the costume is perfect enough so that as it hangs on the wearer, unfastened, the two halves of the snaps that go together fall opposite each other. Did you ever do up a whole line of buttons and find you had started one buttonhole off at the top? It can be done with snaps, too.

This kind of breakaway is most used in musicals, and the usual situation is where there is an opaque overgarment, often long, that will come off quickly to disclose a shorter, transparent, and most often sexy undergarment—plus a great deal of the wearer's figure. It is also possible to have a situation calling for somewhat the same specifications in the drama, though the second sight is not usually so filmy, lacy, or down to such an irreducible minimum.

Runner-up to the snap-out-of-it garment is the wraparound. This is at its best when your performer needs to get into something in a hurry, since here the action is to put out your arms, have the dresser slide the sleeves over them, and then start running for the stage while you tie the sash that holds the garment together around you. If this description leaves too much to the imagination, go to any store that carries Swirls in the housedress section and get a demonstration. Then remember that the design is not patentable, only the name. You, too, can make a wraparound.

The other two expedients for the quick-changer, aside from turning his back to the audience, taking a straw boater off the grand piano of his accompanist, and emerging as a Maurice Chevalier imitation, are underdressing or overdressing. By the latter I do not mean wearing too formal clothes to a party. Quite literally, you underdress by wearing the next costume, or part of it, under what you wear on first, as you would wear underwear. Same principle with overdressing, except it is—as with a topcoat—on the top of the next costume.

In the legitimate theatre the need for this quick-change artistry comes from the desire to maintain the tempo of the play. This might seem to operate in direct reverse of stage directions. If a character announces that he is "going upstairs to change clothes" he has more actual time in which to perform this act than if the play is an episodic one, with ten years between scenes. In the first instance, the author has probably not called for a reappearance of that particular character until he has had, actually, time to change whatever is required. But if the curtain goes down and rises on a scene that involves a longer span of time, such as Ten Years Later, or The Following Morning, the actor has no more time to alter his garb than is required, by the stage manager's timing, to do whatever has to be done to the set. Sometimes this can be as little as forty-five seconds.

When it is a question of a running script, the rule of thumb, as we've mentioned before, is that one allows a minute to the author's page. With the dropped curtain or blackout, the time information must come from either the scene designer, who will know what he is aiming at, or the stage manager, who has clocked it. Whichever it is, stay on your own toes, and keep spry.

Let us be exact and narrow in. In the matter of quick-changes, underdressing refers to a situation in which the actor goes on in Scene One wearing all or part of his costuming for Scene Two underneath his costume for the purpose of effecting as rapid a change as possible. This, we hope, without the knowledge of the spectator. There is another situation in which the term is used—to refer to undergarment, such as when the line of an actor's shorts shows through his trousers, a common fault, or if we can see the end point of a woman's slip under her dress. Stage lighting tends to increase this visibility, and it is not favorably considered. Here the audience does not want to be taken into confidence. It is more apt to think it is fun to be fooled.

Overdressing is just what the word implies. Instead of taking it off, you leave the stage long enough to pile it on. The easiest way to do this is with some regulation outer garment, if script and sense will permit, such as a raincoat, topcoat, or dressing gown. This kind of thing will effect a change with a simple shrug of the shoulders and a cinch of the belt, and almost anyone can do it in the dark, which is what backstage usually is at these points. Or if the outer "coating" just isn't possible, bulky sweaters and voluminous skirts or slacks can be yanked on over slimmer stalks—and I do mean yanked in some cases.

The trouble with both these quick-change devices is that they add bulk, as you can imagine, and you will rarely find an actor or actress who can take much more of this than nature has already provided. God give you slim subjects or a fat bundle of Metrecal stock. Once I had such a series of quick ones that I had to underdress the underdressing, three layers in all. If you have ever been in Los Angeles you may be familiar with a little traffic conglomerate of under- and overpasses known as The Stack. I always think of this whenever I have to do a pileup of clothes. However endowed originally, actresses thus accoutered can be said to be well stacked.

Clothes worn under other clothes always manage to emerge looking as if they had been slept in. Some muss much more than others, of course, and here is where a knowledge of fabric behavior is a great help. Crease and increase are the twin danger points. You can't put the should-be-crisp cotton under a heavy woolen and maintain any reputation for neatness, even to get that dispatch.

For some reason it seems easier to do an abracadabra with men's wear than women's. The lower half of that gray flannel suit is a pretty close approximation of gray flannel slacks, which with the addition of the right spicing can become an entirely different kettle of fish. Whip off the jacket, remove the four-in-hand, and undo a couple of buttons on the shirt. Put on a long-sleeved pullover sweater and, as the actor is walking back onstage, have him undo the two buttons of the button-down shirt and yank the tabs out over the sweater for an even sportier effect. "Ping-Pong, anyone?" An agile actor can do this in well under a minute, which is usually fast enough to suit any director. If he hasn't time to remove the tie and tamper with the shirt fastenings, slap a terry towel around his neck as an ascot, and presto!

One of the reasons men are faster than women is the hair situation. If a woman has changed her clothing, chances are her hair is going to need at least a going-over, perhaps even a change of pace. From piled up on top of her head to hanging down her back, for instance. A man only needs a quick swipe with a comb through that quarter inch of foliation on top of him, if that.

Sometimes a change will be required between the scenes within an act simply to indicate the passage of time. Scene One has closed with our heroine resplendent in a formal evening gown. Scene Two reveals her in a flowing negligee, pouring coffee. Obviously the morning after, though what morning and after what is perhaps not always so clear. Or the man who has exited in a snap brim reenters carrying a straw boater. Ah ha, a change of season. It must be spring, at least, or even summer.

Why can't the audience find out all this by simply reading the program? So they could, if they only would. But either audiences come to the theatre because they can't read, and so are denied the entertainment value of curling up with a good book, or it's against the rules of the game they are playing, making up their own rules as they go along. Reading in the program that it is the same living room, six months later, early morning, would not be fair. It would, in some way, alter their handicaps. It might also help, unfairly, in understanding the play. So the costume designer gives a jog to the memory, or does some handwriting on the wall, or pulls a rabbit out of an Easter bonnet to indicate what's going on, when!

The most and quickest changes in my own theatrical experience occurred in *Two for the Seesaw*. This play had many scenes within the acts, and each scene change represented a time span that had elapsed, so that it began with an altered set of circumstances. An alteration of costumes was essential. George Jenkins had done a miraculous job on the settings, which went from the man's to the girl's apartment or vice versa in a matter of seconds, literally. By using both a wagon and a revolving stage he actually made this transition over what appeared to be several city blocks in a minute, a minute and a half, or two minutes, depending on whether he had simply to pull one set into place with the wagon stage apparatus, or both pull and revolve a set to show a new angle of the apartment.

Even with all these wonders, the pace, as rehearsals in the set began, was not fast enough to suit George, the director Arthur Penn, or the stage manager. They all sat or stood around with stopwatches, timing changes, and they agreed that it all needed to be faster. If you have twelve scene changes, each running a minute too long, you have added a dozen minutes of dead weight time to a play, a dozen occasions in which you can lose the audience's attention and involvement. Of course each time the cry rang out—*Faster!*—it meant that Anne Bancroft had to project herself into a new costume that much more speedily. She was a quick girl, and willing, but after all, she didn't do *The Miracle Worker* until a few years later. As for myself, I was beginning to feel as if my two actors were harnessed to one of the chariots in *Ben Hur,* while I cracked the whip.

One of the most effective things about all this is that the curtain never went down during a scene change. The lights simply blacked out, although not completely, as a panorama of the New York skyline above the top edge of the back wall of the set twinkled into a little distracting prominence. Nor could Anne leave the stage during all the pushing and pulling. It simply wasn't safe with all that going on. So she stood on about a foot and a half of either a wagon or a wheel, with Ray, the wardrobe mistress, crouching beside her in the dark, while their base of operations moved into another section of the stage area, and Anne changed from leotards to pajamas or street clothes or tucked a tea towel into her belt to serve as a cooking apron. They were both brave women. Luckily, Ray soon had provided an adequate stock of first-aid items as necessary to that backstage as her needle and thread. Anne was supposed to have an ulcer, according to the script, but whether true or false, she picked up a few on the outside of shins, hips, and other vulnerable spots almost nightly. This was one of those plays where there was overdressing under overdressing. At one point Anne wore three layers of clothing. Fortunately she had the figure to stand all that padding. Or do I mean just fortunately she had a figure? Like on that opening night in Washington that might have got us closed. . . .

There was one scene when Henry Fonda leaves, late at night but forgets his hat and comes back for it. He rings the downstairs bell to the apartment to be admitted, and then in the time it takes to climb to the floor Anne lived on, she was supposed to get into the striped man's pajamas the character of Gittel Mosca affected. These were kept in a partly visible little chest in a small dressing room that was half offstage. When Anne opened the drawer and took them out, she dropped the lower half. She had to come onstage and open the door wearing exactly half her costume, which would, if it had lacked another half inch, have been shorter than the law allows. She looked awfully cute, and we all wanted to leave the business that way, but we were afraid to. Whatever censor was covering the play that night must have been looking the other way for just that one moment, or he could, in that day, have closed the show. Nothing could guarantee that he would wink at us twice.

That was a found show. No reason why not. Mr. Fonda wore his own clothes, and Gittel was supposed to be a girl with very little money and no really recherché taste. Most of her clothes came from the sportswear and junior departments of Bonwit's. The clothes were not spectacular, but they fitted the play well enough so that when, after a year's hard wear, the final scene dress just wore out, the management wanted one exactly like the original.

Did you ever have to buy from a store a dress they were

featuring a year ago? Underwear, a sweater, even shoes, perhaps yes. But a year-old dress from a specialty shop, which means a very fashionable resource that prides itself on being up to date? Just try. I did, sure before I started that my effort was hopeless. Not at all. The manufacturer had no more in stock, true, but he did have enough material on his shelves for two more of that model. If I would buy not one, but two dresses, so he could clear out that end of fabric, he would disrupt his production line enough to cut two specials and put them into work. I had to decide while he was on the phone —that minute. Reviewing how much money I probably had in my bank account, and how I would look in a size twelve —I take a sixteen—I said yes. Then I had to go out and persuade management that it really ought to cover itself adequately by owning two of those dresses for Anne.

I must have gotten out of bed on the right side that morning, since for the second time that day I got "yes" for an answer, this time from producer Fred Coe. Start to finish, I loved working on *Two for the Seesaw*. I had believed in the play since the first time I read the script. The scene designer was not only a friend but one of the very best designers I know. The producer was a lovely man who stayed on the coast until a day or so before we went out of town for the tryout, so he was no problem, and Arthur Penn, the new director, looked like an up and coming genius. It was a full-time job, but can you think of any better way of filling your time?

16

Just When to Kill Yourself

One of New York's leading theatrical photographers, who has taken pictures of everyone from Helen Hayes to Princess Grace of Monaco, has a saying known to all his friends. When someone asks Marcus Blechman how he is, if he has had a bad day, he says that he is about to kill himself. This means that the retoucher has spoiled the proofs, that he ran out of the right kind of film in the middle of a sitting, or that he thought he had a chance to photograph Marlene Dietrich but that it had fallen through again. There are two women he still hasn't taken pictures of who are important to Marcus, and Dietrich is sixty percent of them. At any rate, he can't be very serious about his suicide plans, since he has been making this threat for over twenty-five years, and he is still alive.

So, when *do* you kill yourself? I should say:

1. If you have whistled in a dressing room on opening night.

2. If you have tossed your hat on a bed. Particularly if you have been *seen* tossing your hat on that bed.

3. If you have been guilty of putting *fresh* flowers on a costume, hat, in an actress's hair, or otherwise used them on stage.

These are three theatrical superstitions that are as current among members of the profession as their Equity cards. I have burrowed into the minds of various acting friends for their origins, and come up with answers for two of them. I shall rest with my two-thirds majority, unless someone fills me in before this is committed to print. The whistling bit comes from the very old days before there were real dressing rooms, and changes of costume were simply made offstage. If an actor whistled, it might be heard right through the star's speech. Bad luck for this actor, then, since it was quite apt to get him fired.

The hat on the bed is still a mystery. The fresh-flower taboo is simply a matter of common sense. Flowers fade, wilt, and shed leaves and petals as they get devitalized by the heat from a theatre's battery of lights. Aside from looking their worst after they have been exposed to all this torture, they become dangerous. One spilled orchid petal on the floor of a stage is as great a hazard as a banana peel, but it is against the rules to stop and pick one up. So tuck a nice silk carnation in that actor's buttonhole. If you insist on realism, you can buy them now made of feathers, but perfumed with the scent of the real thing.

In all circumstances other than the three listed above, it is better to stay alive in the face of calamity. Nine times out of ten you will be the only person around who can undo the damage. Instead of the cyanide capsule that dissolves so quickly in the mouth of the apprehended criminal, much better carry with you an extra reserve of energy, all the ingenuity you can muster, and possibly a handful of Benzedrine, or whatever pill you are on. Something that will help you work while everyone else is asleep.

Just to give a rough idea of what the designer can endure and still survive, here is a small collection of horror stories out of the wardrobe closet. None of them made a skeleton out of me, though at times I felt, while I was going through it, as if one foot was on a tightrope and the other in a grave.

One play, *Hide and Seek,* had an atomic-bomb sequence in it. During the "scare" part, ten or eleven characters had to don antiradiation clothing, radiation-proof, that is. I hadn't the faintest idea what this looked like, but my job was to find out and reproduce it by the dozen. However, I did have connections, or one, an architect who had worked on the construction of Brookhaven and he still knew a few people out there. By dint of proceeding cautiously through channels and with more character references than I had dreamed I could muster, permission was obtained for me to examine and lay hands on, not the very latest antiradiation protective cover, but at least, the one before the last. This had already been superseded, but it still looked like something from outer space to a layman. After pulling every conceivable wire I got an OK to have these reproduced, and even for my maskmaker, who was going to do something elaborate with papier-mâché for the headgear, to get a quick look. The body covering was to be constructed out of a stiff drill into a jump suit kind of thing and then be sprayed for additional stiffness;

there were special high boots and long gloves to be made, all very expensive. All complicated, exhausting, difficult, but at least I knew that what I was reproducing was authentic in appearance.

We left town for Wilmington, where the first dress rehearsal was to be. I drove down, as the coverings took up a whole Ford sedan to transport. Handling my treasures as if they were rare thousand-year-old eggs, I got the outfits to the theatre and my actors into them. As the curtain went up on the last act of dress rehearsal, somewhere around one A.M., I slid, depleted of strength but proud, into the seat next to the director, expecting at least a Distinguished Service Cross for the wonders I had wrought. Not a bit of it.

Reggie Denham blew his top. The masterpieces wouldn't do at all. Not for a minute. I assured him that they were exactly right and outlined my bona fides. No, and again no. They didn't look like what an audience would expect them to look like. Period. Now, whip up something else, please. And quickly. We open in three nights . . .

When rehearsal was over I crawled upstairs—the theatre is in the hotel—to bed but not to sleep. My brain raced futilely all night.

In the morning, staring disconsolately at the breakfast menu, I read the name across the top—DuPont Hotel. Suddenly my brain cleared. The DuPont Company was, God bless them, in the business of chemicals. Thank all the saints for a company town! I gulped the last swallow of coffee and made for the telephone.

How many calls it took, beginning with public relations, until I got the right men and all the OK's I never counted.

That total was on my per diem expense account. But by early forenoon I was on the company bus headed for whatever storage center housed the supply of reserve chemists' masks. There were several shapes and sizes to choose from, and after experiments to be sure the actors could still be heard delivering their speeches through all the paraphernalia, I emerged with a sample mask on loan and its source and number. It got a fast OK from Reggie, was tried on and sampled by four or five actors, and I got started on the elaborate business of ordering from a supply company who thought all theatre people were crazy, and this proved it.

Replacing the lower part, the suit, of the costume was silly it was so simple. I needed something for both men and women, available in all sizes, that was uniform. I located a wholesale supplier of waiters', busboys', and waitresses' uniforms, went over there with the measurement list I always carry in my money belt, and went to town. A friendly prop man at the theatre helped save the day, or night, by swiping paint from the scenery department and we sprayed them army drab, which looked terribly official. The costumes were successful I might add, but the play was not.

Another story involves some business about shoes. The leading lady in this case had extremely small and pretty feet, and the best was none too good for setting them off. After combing the New York market unsuccessfully for a pair of shoes that would do—her small size was so rare as to be unavailable—we finally ordered a pair from Europe for her opening scene. It was a near thing, but they were flown in the day before we were to leave town for the tryout. I opened the precious box, saw the trim brown alligator, and inspected the inside of one shoe. Size four and a half B. Correct.

The first night out of town I was summoned peremptorily to our Number One dressing room. The leading lady sat with one shoe off, one on, in a temper that was not acted. "Look at this," she said, and handed me both shoes, soles together. One was a good half inch shorter than the other. "I can't even get into it!" she wailed.

We tried everything to stretch that shoe, but relasting is not too effective with alligator, which is one of the reasons it wears so well. We finally got it to a size where she could get into it, but it was torture, and she couldn't keep it on for more than five minutes. She was making her first entrance with a limp.

And if you can't buy a four and a half alligator pump in New York, just try to do it in New Haven. There were no brown shoes at all in that size, and the actress's own shoe wardrobe, since it was still summer, and hot, ran from white to sand. The director was acid. "What's the matter, darling? Can't you even walk on straight?"

About a half-hour before opening-night curtain I had an idea, and sat in the dressing room outlining it to the leading lady as she outlined her lips. Then I rushed out front to watch.

She made her first entrance loaded with bundles, supposedly exhausted from a shopping spree. Business was for her to sink down on the center-stage couch and sigh with relief. Tonight she stretched out on the couch full length, surreptitiously wriggled one foot out of a shoe, and let it fall to the floor. Then she sighed. Every woman in the audience laughed. So did some of the men.

She got two more laughs out of the shoe business. One was when to answer the phone she tried to find the shoe, couldn't get into it fast enough, and eventually made a dash for the instrument, half shod and walking unevenly. The last came as she was preparing to leave the scene to change her clothes and she just made a few faces as she put that shoe back on. That business stayed in for the run, which was a long one. Luckily the play was a comedy.

Time out for a digression. If you don't have the time, skip this section. It is highly noneducational. It takes us simply from the feet of clay of one actress to the more alabaster limbs of another. How true it is I cannot say, I got it strictly on hearsay evidence. Margot Stevenson told it to me while she was standing by in *Venus Observed,* and one of the lovely principal players in that Fry play was Lili Palmer. If you don't know how beautiful Miss Palmer is, you may have missed seeing Bob Ardrey's first movie, *Thunder Rock*. That excellent movie was a flop when first released, but it did, right from the beginning, show off Miss Palmer's beauty from head to toe.

One night Marlene Dietrich came to see *Venus,* and having friends in the cast, went visiting backstage afterward. When Miss Dietrich with her famous legs got to Miss Palmer's dressing room, she sat down for a real chat, complimenting Lili on her performance, which had been excellent. Then, as women will, they got down to basics, the wardrobe, which had been designed by Valentina. Miss Dietrich, certainly an authority on the subject, was even gracious enough to say the nicest things about the clothes, which were superb, ". . . except for those shoes, darling. They are terrible."

"Terrible," said Lili Palmer, "why I like them. Good-looking, and even comfortable, too. My friends say they look very nice from out front."

"Just give me one of them," ordered Legs Dietrich. Reaching for the shoe box, she kicked off her footgear and slipped her own feet into Palmer's stage shoes. Then, leaning back in the chair, she extended her feet, arches curved, toes pointing down, the most becoming position for a lady's feet.

"See!" she said triumphantly, pointing to her pedal extremities, "just like I said, they are horrible shoes. Even on *me,* they look terrible!" Which is certainly putting one foot before another. Was the best foot forward?

Ever since really settling down to what I wanted to do for a living, I had an irrepressible itch to design the clothing for at least one movie. The size of the audience reached by the cinema was part of the allure, so was the size of Hollywood salaries. Such West Coast friends as I had who were set designers or decorators could anticipate a sort of hungry and drooling dog look on my face whenever they referred to a new job with the boredom that comes from familiarity and such high on the hog living. They were kindness itself, they all tried, but it was years before Harry Horner was able to phone me that I mustn't lose any sleep, but maybe, maybe, there was just a possibility. . . .

I was in Hollywood at the time, and after losing sleep for about three weeks, the moment came when I was due on the next lap of my vacation, which was to lead to Taos, New Mexico, on the way back to New York. On the day before departure I spoke to Harry to see if he had any news, but he was still waiting for his own contract to be signed and some more of the money to come in. I did find out that the movie was to be made in Mexico, one of my favorite places to go, and that the period was circa the 1860s. Since I was an early Civil War buff the whole project became desirable beyond expression. I left Harry everything I could think of in the way of phone numbers and forwarding addresses, and left, feet dragging, for New Mexico.

When I got there I found a playscript waiting for me to read, sent by a New York producer who planned an early fall opening on Broadway, and who wanted an immediate yea or nay, and my almost as immediate presence in his office. I read the script, but it wasn't half as funny as the author intended. It didn't even seem worthwhile cutting a vacation short for, and the money wasn't more than bread and butter, while the Hollywood thing was real jam (or George).

I stalled as long as I could, and gained a few extra days by refusing to leave without a signed contract in my pocket, but airmail was never quicker or more efficient. Just before signing the contract I phoned Harry again. Still, no news. And, since a woman must eat and I had a desire to maintain my then weight, I picked up any old ball point, hoping it wouldn't write, and signed away the next two months of my life. Then I drove as slowly as I could without killing the engine up to the post office and dropped the envelope containing the contract in the slot.

The phone was not ringing as I came back from the post office, nor did it ring all that day. It wasn't until the next morning that Harry called to say it was all set, and how fast could I get there? I had to tell him that I was on my way to the airport, all right, but that the plane I would be taking would land at LaGuardia, not L.A. International. You don't try to get out of a signed contract, not if you were brought up by my grandfather. That really was one of the times I wanted to kill myself. But instead of writing a suicide note I began making a wardrobe list of requirements as soon as the plane took off from Albuquerque.

The theatre is like that, once you get going in it. There is always the hour of decision. You can be out of work for months, and then, if one job comes along, there will be another at the same time, so that you have to make a choice. Ask any actor, you will find this overlapping one of the headaches of his career. The thing I most wish for all theatre people is, I guess, enough basic financial security so that when that moment of choice comes, the job can be chosen because it is the right job, not because it will buy the next meal quicker. That choice is a luxury not open to many along Broadway.

17

The Other Roads to Rome

The population explosion and overcrowding is not confined to the main body of New York City itself. This disease has spread from the larger arteries to the tributary veins and blood vessels of the theatrical profession. Local 829 is just as crowded as any other union, perhaps even more than most. If you are determined to design costumes, and don't feel like getting involved in this traffic jam, or if, for any other reason, the life of a Broadway designer doesn't quite meet with your ideas of the good life, what can you do about it?

Being a costume designer is not like being a doctor, or a lawyer or a teacher. There is always some place where there is a shortage of personnel in these three categories. But as a costume designer, by and large you will have to function in New York or Hollywood, and these two towns are well staffed with your competition. Since it has come up, however, perhaps this is a good time to consider the alternates. . . .

For one thing, you can be a costume designer by avocation instead of vocation. This means you will do it in your spare time, as some people go in for deep sea fishing or Sunday painting. And it will take care of your spare time. Once involved, you probably won't have any left over.

If you live in a reasonably civilized community these days, there is probably a community theatre within driving distance. Most of these theatres have a plethora of would-be acting talent, but there is often a dearth of people to do the work behind the scenes; the work that doesn't make a personal appearance, and that still requires knowledge or training. Volunteer your services for one play, and if you like it and they like you, you will probably have a job. Besides, it's a good way to get to know your neighbors.

Assembling the clothes for this kind of operation is usually done by scrounging. You go to the best nearby store or shop for the purpose and offer them program credit, and a line in the newspaper if you can get it, in exchange for the right to borrow enough merchandise for your purpose. There will be a limit on the number of times these clothes are to be worn, as they most likely will have to be returned to stock. As a rule, your problem will only be to arrange for women's apparel. Men will be willing to wear their own coats and suits, but it is a good idea to start with the stipulation that you are to be given some chance at selecting which ones. Otherwise you may find every man in the company turning up in his gray flannel.

If the production is to be a costume play, you will first have to do some researching, and then you will find yourself running a workroom of amateur seamstresses. Look for the best among these volunteers, give these best the hardest work, naturally, and grapple them to your soul with hoops of steel, or handcuff them to their sewing machines, whichever seems most feasible. You will have a use for everybody, from people who can make crowns and wands out of cardboard, to someone to paint last year's summer sandals gold, to that little woman who has learned to make death masks out of plaster of paris. But for the ass's head in *Midsummer Night's Dream* I suggest you take up a collection and rent same from a regular costume company. Money spent on a very few rented extras of this sort goes a long way toward giving a professional slant to the whole show, and you can perform these miracles by mail, if need be.

The sad part about this kind of work is the amount of effort you will all put into something that is only scheduled to run for one, two, or three performances. Oh well, remember, shows have closed on Broadway just as quickly, and with worse notices, I am sure.

Another alternative to Broadway professionalism is to take refuge in the halls of ivy. More and more colleges and universities are opening Fine Arts or Drama Departments. Often these have new theatres with jewel box construction and excellent modern equipment. When the Drama Department is large enough there will be a dramatic coach or teacher, set designer, and a costume supervisor, though in some of the smaller colleges the last two named will have to double in brass. There are usually about four productions a year that are full scale, one each quarter, tri-semester, or whatever, depending on the scholastic year. Except for a period of flurry just before each play, there is not too much danger of overwork, since the more academic of the other instructors are apt to make certain demands of their own on student time.

This is not the direct road to affluence, since a teacher's salary is paid for ten months of the year, and it is up to the instructor to budget himself so that this can be spread over twelve months. Salaries vary from state to state, and often depend on the endowment existing for the department. If you are capable of working all year round, it is often possible to "teach" the summer session too, thereby increasing your yearly take. Often, too, the summer students are the ones most serious about their theatrical ambitions, and you may get your most interesting and hopeful projects during the summer. You do not need to be a member of the union for either this or the community theatre work.

What you do need for the college jobs of course is a certain academic tidbit known as a degree. In drama or art, preferably drama. And preferably from one of the universities with a strong department, such as Carnegie Tech or the Workshop at Yale. So if you find yourself leaning toward those halls of academe, *stay in school*. The promotions come faster—the salaries start going up in direct proportion to the number of letters after your name, and as soon as possible, write a book, any old book, pertinent or not. You'll never make head of department unless you do.

Where do the costumes you will design come from? Good question. All over the lot would be a fair answer. Some are scrounged, as in the previously described community theatres, or at least they were when I worked in my own university. Nowadays these Drama Departments have become so dignified that scrounging may be frowned on. There is usually a certain budget for each production's clothes, often derived from the sale of tickets to the performance or performances. And many college and even lower-school theatres are trying to build up a wardrobe department that will provide a backlog from which to work, and are now very gracious indeed about accepting old ermine wraps and pretty little ball gowns their original owners once wore when attached to the embassy at Graustark or when being presented at the Court of St. James.

And part of the time it's just stitch, stitch, stitch. Volunteers from the drama classes who haven't made the tryout are gladly accepted. The boys paint the scenery, the girls run the machines, although you may find a reversal of roles sometimes brings better results. And some schools have been known to engage a Mistress of the Wardrobe who is not above lifting a finger.

Next—the summer stock companies. This won't give you a full-time occupation, but it may be all you can take. Another warning—putting a venturesome foot into the countryside may force you into taking a giant step back toward Broadway. You may be a rebel, but this is union territory. You can work as an apprentice, usually unpaid, under a legally authorized member of 829, but if you want to get to any place in authority, you will have to join.

I once worked in summer stock for a producer whose only connection with the theatre was this company, which he ran every year. Rumor had it that the operation was successful enough so that he could live the rest of the year on the summer's take. For all I know, of course, he may have had private financing, such as a family who took him in as soon as the snow fell. At any rate, he ran a very fine summer outfit, and his theatre was considered one of *the* places to go. But just to show you that Massachusetts is not such a far cry from New York, it is alleged that when he moved into town, opened an office in the Broadway vicinity, and began to rally forces and investment money for a play in the city, his country performances had won him such favor among the angels that the coin of the realm rolled in.

What is the system for working the straw-hat circuit? There are probably as many systems as there are theatres, but a great change has come in with the "traveling package." In summer stock the actors are responsible for their own wardrobes, and in the spots where the audiences were more interested in circuses than bread, a pretty face and trunks and trunks of ready-to-wear got one further than acting talent. From some of the "packages" that do very well in this year of Our Lord, I cannot see that this method of casting has been declared unconstitutional. . . .

One summer I helped an actress who was going to Elitch's Gardens in Denver to play star and lead parts get ready for the excursion. She knew some of the plays she would be doing, but had no firm commitment on all of them. There was to be nine or ten plays, I have forgotten now just how many, and we went through her wardrobe, selecting the proper things for the parts we were sure of, occasionally buying a new dress when nothing she owned seemed right. But what would she need for those unknown plays? The way things were running, she was averaging four outfits per drama. Raising the ante to five, just in case, we selected clothing suitable for a leading lady, at least, with a couple of real starry ensembles on the chance that they might throw a Gertrude Lawrence type part at her. In all, she bought twenty-five new outfits, some of them ensembles, all with shoes and bags suitable for appearance onstage. Thank heaven, she could make a very professional hat if it turned out she needed one. In all we did forty-three outfits, none of which could be worn around Denver until they had first been used in a play, or the surprise would be lost. She said that the first few weeks she was afraid to wear anything but a dressing gown, even to do the marketing.

We loaded her onto the train—she had way too much luggage to be able to afford flying—and I followed her out on my way to California several weeks later. I spent a week in Denver and found her happy but a bit harassed, and we sorted out clothes for the rest of the season, which was scheduled by now. During the summer she bought two or three dresses locally, which is poor policy since every woman in the audience knew where the dress came from, how much it cost, and had probably tried it on. They wanted *new* New York clothes. At the end of the season she came to my place, triumphant though exhausted. It looked as if she would be asked back next summer. "But do you know what? I'm going to need at least ten more outfits than I had this year! All of them new. I can't take anything they have seen before. Meanwhile, how in the world am I going to wear out all these ball gowns? Job-hunting for the fall season?" Which was, of course, her little problem. . . .

But the space age is beginning to change all that. Now, instead of playing ten parts in one place, a star plays one part in ten places, or perhaps only five, depending on her draw and her package's booking agent. She can wear the same clothes in Miami that she wore in New Hope. A production, including all *principal* players is all set up and costumed in New York, and only the smaller parts, bit players and mob scenes, are filled in at the grass roots. This is still done from the actor's own clothes closet, unless the play is a costume one, and in cases like that the traveling package carries around a more extensive part of the cast, if not all of it. No wonder repertory is on the wane.

Sometimes a summer playhouse will be used to try out a new play to see if it looks likely for fall production in town, but that's a whole different story and leads back to Broadway.

Having wandered back into the purlieus of Broadway professionalism, let's make a frontal attack. What are the more closely related alternates to designing for the New York theatre that may bypass some of the disadvantages? The first that leaps to mind is to work in pictures or for television. Notice I don't say Hollywood, since that would not be the sole area of your activities by a long shot. A contract to do motion pictures has become the same as enlisting in the Navy—join and see the world. It is now more likely that you will be working in Italy or Egypt or England or Tokyo than on the West Coast.

The best thing about pictures and TV is the pay, which soars to astronomical pinnacles. Few studios have permanently contracted-for costume departments, and they are forced to higher salaries with the loss of contract personnel. Which seems fair enough. But if you are working on a cinema, the period of paid employment is usually longer, and if you are working on *Cleopatra* it may seem forever. Just settle down in Rome and get paid for it. The only trouble you should have is with the income-tax people. . . .

As the rewards increase, so does the inaccessability of the jobs. For one thing, the young designer will be bucking names. With the cost of cinema productions sounding like the sum required to finance space exploration, the producer or studio has to be sure that every facet of his picture is in the best hands available to his multimillion-dollar project. The Broadway producer is more of a gambling man at heart —either that or his backers leave more to his talent for discovery than does a bank that is lending the money for a picture, and whose stockholders are looking forward to a nice dividend this year. Although on Broadway you can often start at the top, in the movies it is usually necessary to begin as an assistant to an assistant sketcher, or maybe even by sharpening pencils for that assistant to an assistant. If years spent at this kind of working your way up do not break your spirit so badly that you lose faith in your own designing ability, it is a fine way to learn your trade.

More and more the movies are becoming designed rather than found shows. Finding, in Hollywood, was only a way of saving money for those cheapies, the one- or two-hundred-thousand-dollar-budget picture. By the same token, places that do the execution for movie designers are becoming more and more self contained, and can produce anything required from head to toe. Naturally they have their own millinery departments, but one thing that made my own Broadway mouth water as much as does the California abalone was a whole row of cobbler's benches with shoemakers actually handcrafting the little colored boots for the chorus of the film version of *Carousel,* each in an analogous shade of pale kid. It was a luxury I couldn't afford for most leading ladies in New York. Like Madame Chanel, I love Luxe.

On the other hand television, though it runs parallel to the movies in many respects, is largely a findings business. Only the big spectaculars are designed, and not all of these. Often a big star will get a dress—sometimes on loan for the program credit—from her favorite couturier.

But the routine television show with the faithful secretary ordering up sandwiches for her overworked boss, or the lady accomplice or the innocent widow or bereft baby, becomes a question of making out a costume plot, and then getting everything together the day before yesterday. Perhaps, if it is a period series, there is a contract with a costume company, on whom the show calls endlessly for frontier clothes, Civil War uniforms, or whatever is "wanted in emergency" in ward thirty-three. Live or tape, the production has to operate on schedule, and the costume companies I know are very cooperative and helpful, often abandoning regular Broadway clients when the call comes through on the loudspeaker, and leaving them lost between Etruscan Footgear and Striped Garb, Men. One of the reasons the TV designer is always a little frenetic is that it is so often difficult to get a final, completed, and positively definite copy of the script in time to get together with the various actors who are located anywhere from Connecticut to a little farm near Philadelphia, in time for fittings.

If it is a modern found show and has been running for several weeks with a cast of regulars, the situation is simpler. You will have most of the important players' sizes, and you will know a fair amount about their tastes and what is right for the show. If you work regularly with one or two stores, these suppliers will be familiar with your requirements and not panic at your own distraught sortie on their stocks. Regular salespeople for this can be a big help and save you precious hours you will need whenever there is a guest star who requires special attention.

If you are working for a network you may only be assigned to one show as a staff designer. If you are put on more shows, you will be paid accordingly, and the temptation is often to say "yes" to more work than you can do well. Or if you are working for the company who makes the "soaps" and provides them to the network, your original contract may be, for instance, for two of the shows they make. This is not too difficult once you have learned the ropes and gathered momentum, since often you can do several things at the same time, such as shoes, bags, gloves, ties, and lingerie for both on one trip.

Taking a pas or deux north from Broadway, we ran into the corps de ballet. Moving uptown into this rarefied atmosphere can be a dizzying experience, like suddenly finding oneself in a spot eight or nine thousand feet above sea level. Designing costumes for a ballet brings designing, in my opinion, as close to being an art form as it is ever likely to get.

The past couple of decades have done much to revolutionize the whole ballet, and nowhere has the new freedom been more apparent than in the costuming. Instead of the conventional white tutu, think of the now accepted cowboy clothing of *Rodeo,* or the symbolic dressing of *Seven Deadly Sins.* From the point of view of the beginner, while this breakthrough may make ballet designing more mouth-watering, it also makes it more difficult. Competition is not only professional, it includes the names of big-time artists, real ones, such as Berman, Berard, Chagall, and Noguchi. Also, there is a solidifying trend toward the whole ballet being under the guiding hand of one designer, who does both sets and costumes. So here, unless you qualify in both departments, chances grow slim though not impossible. But ballet is not a large field. How many new, from the ground cloth up, ballets do we have each year, costumed in America?

There is another qualification that ballet requires, and not a temperamental one. You must know something, at least, about music. Here you do not first read the script, you learn the score. And if you know music well enough to read it, so much the better.

One of the reasons I say ballet designing comes close to art is that here the designer shares the stage more openly with the other performing members of the company. The orchestra is there, of course, but in the pit. Onstage, at least, the entire performance is visual, and if the action were to "freeze" at any minute, as sometimes it comes close to doing, if you will think about it, the audience expects that frozen moment to present a beautiful and satisfying picture. And the designer's contribution to this picture is no small one.

A knowledge of anatomy is almost essential. In ballet, from the design point of view, the word "articulation," so common to balletomanes, means talking with the body, not just hands and feet, but all of it. You must preserve this freedom to speak in the clothes you design, and see that it is delivered in the execution. This is no polite minor request, it is an imperative. You must know about shoulders and knees and thighs and how they work, and what they are capable of after years of rigorous training. To limit, by the costuming, anything the dancer's body could do naked, would be tantamount to murder. One of the best ways to be sure you do not commit this sin would be to know the actual construction of the costuming, as well as the designing.

There is another field of designing that may be to your liking, and that is full of variety. It could take you anywhere from a high school auditorium to a nightclub. This is the business of doing costumes for singles—dancers, monologists—for doubles—a man and woman team, or a pair of dancers—on up to a whole dance act or troupe. I loved this work, and it supported me for a long time before I broke into the theatre proper. It also brought in many good contacts. As performers grow more famous and successful, they often carry along with them people who were helpful when they were unknown.

My work began when a mutual friend brought me a young dancer who had recently appeared in *Jubilee,* and who was now booked into the Club Versailles. Her name was Dorothy Fox, and her partner was a young man named Chuck Walters, better known later on as a very successful director and producer of musicals in Hollywood. These youngsters needed a lot of clothes, had no money, and could Dorothy pay me off as Versailles paid her? I was eating at the time, which was all that mattered, so I said yes. She has been paying off ever since, for now I go out to California and spend my summers with her and her husband in their beautiful home in Pacific Palisades.

Dorothy needed, to begin with, a long, concealing, and yet fluid and sexy garment that would break away and reveal the gorgeous figure hampered by nothing but a minimum of black lace. I said yes, not having the foggiest notion what a breakaway was. But I learn quickly, and in a week I was not only throwing the word into my own conversations with the less erudite than I, I was also busily making one.

Doing these costumes provided a great deal of information about what the dance field requires, and so I learned by trial and error, with the team of Fox and Walters being very patient. Since I am almost as dance-struck as I am stagestruck, this was valuable training. For one thing, costumes may break apart, when and where intended, but they must never come apart. Sew them with fine steel wire if you have to, and see that they are inspected for weaknesses after every wearing. If the dancers are energetic, and what ones aren't these days, the strain on the costumes will be tremendous. Don't use, as one very famous designer did, antique lace for the shoulders and tops. It may be very beautiful, but only for one performance. Age could not wither, perhaps, but it could make frail.

Another thing dancers require is that the costume never fall in an ugly or comic line that is unintentional. It cannot get caught or stuck, so that a trouser leg remains looped up, or a sleeve turns back. Adequate fullness will help avoid this, plus a fabric with enough body and suppleness. Stiff fabrics

are the most dangerous, though the Kabuki dancers use
them all the time. However, that is their genius. A fair
substitute for this attribute, and one that is available, is to
weight the seams and hems. Use not only dressmaker weights
but the little upholstery beadlike ones that come by the yard.

One of the pleasant features of the scientific revolution is
that many of today's modern products play right into the
dancer's hands or onto their legs. Whatever you think of
stretch pants on the street, they certainly belong on some
stages and in some clubs on the right figures. Keeping
abreast of these developments may save you a lot of unnecessary work. Places to look for them are, aside from in
those maddening ads that develop an appetite for a product
before it is available, the best fabric counters you know of,
the theatrical fabric suppliers such as Dazians and Maharam,
and the places where dancers buy their shoes, like La Ray
and Capezio. The latter two are apt to have garments made
up, such as stretch pants or leotards, and if you can get your
hands on a piece of what you want, you can usually work
your way back to the source, using that automatic opener of
doors, "For the theatre."

Dancers never came along fast enough to suit me, and it
was several years after I began with Dorothy before I met
Jack Cole. I had been a Cole admirer for a long time, going
to watch him and his dancers wherever they appeared if I
was within hailing distance. That same mutual friend who
had brought me Miss Fox knew Jack, and as soon as he
thought the omens were propitious, he made an engagement
for us both to meet at his place. I pondered what to wear
very seriously and finally decided on a severe but elegant

black with high neck and long sleeves, and a skirt that had more yardage than I had ever managed to get into a dress before. It made a perfect foil to the most exciting thing I owned, a wild hat from Sally Victor that had cost seventy-five dollars wholesale and that I never saw duplicated. It was two hats, really, copied from the Peruvian, and consisted of a large felt overhat on top of a skull-encasing purple jersey shape that tied under my chin, no hair showing. It was folly, but I thought stunning folly, so I set out for the interview as full of as much fear and trepidation as a hat that size could cover. I felt a bit as if I were being looked over for a diplomatic appointment to the Court of St. James.

My conversation was so beguiled as to be banal, I am sure. I couldn't have had a theory about clothes if my life had depended on it. The only smart thing I did was to leave a few minutes before Mr. Cole. After he had left, my friend phoned me at home, where I had gone, nervously drained to exhaustion. I clutched the phone as if it might get away and said, "Well?"

"You've got the job," my friend said.

"How do you know?" I demanded. "Tell me every word."

"After you left, Jack stretched out on the couch. 'She's the tallest woman I ever saw.'" All his dancers were tiny girls. "'But did you see that hat?'" No one could have helped seeing it. I had kept it on all afternoon, since my hair underneath was a shambles. There were only three of us in the room, so it had to be seen.

"What about that hat?" my friend asked him.

"Absolutely mad," Jack asserted. "But she'll do. Anyone

brave enough to put that on her head and go out in the street has what I want in the way of a designer . . ."

You never can tell, can you, where the next job's coming from? Or what's going to cinch it for you.

We began slowly, but I dressed Jack and his troupe of dancers for years after that. I did his opening at the Persian Room, two engagements at Chez Paree in Chicago, and ended on the West Coast with an engagement at Slapsy Maxie's.

Mr. Cole is not only a wonderful dancer and choreographer, he is a very intelligent man, full of ideals, theories, and ideas. Consequently making costumes for him often presented new problems never encountered before. For his return engagement at Chez Paree he wanted to do *Afternoon of a Faun,* wearing costumes that looked like Gauguin's paintings. Research on the paintings was easy enough, but that was not the year fabric manufacturers had discovered Tahitian prints, and there was just no material to be had with the big splashy flowers properly spaced. But you don't tell Jack, or anyone who has a definite idea, "It can't be done." You ask yourself—How can I do it?

For one thing, Jack really wanted those sarongs made of lightweight wool, so we bought yards and yards of a wool crepe in a heavenly light red. Then we bought some curtain stretchers from Macy's and all kinds of paints. Part of the problem was that we wanted not a many-colored flower that would sink into the fabric, but an opaque white passion flower that would stand out clearly and with strength from any part of that huge nightclub. After experimenting, the best paint turned out to be regular artists' oil, apt to dry stiff, and taking days to do that. We stretched the red wool on the curtain dryers that took up most of my living room, and a friend of mine who was an artist went to work. When one section was finished, we moved it along on the rack and proceeded to do another three yards. But it couldn't be moved until it was perfectly dry of course, so we soon found ourselves with two sets of racks, one to paint and one to be drying, and the project usurped my bedroom as well. I breathed in paint and turpentine for weeks.

That *Afternoon* was determined to be a difficult one. The dance required a spear, which I didn't think was woman's work, and had ordered to be made and shipped by one of the costume companies. When it arrived in Chicago where the group was rehearsing, two days before the opening, it was broken. Jack phoned me in New York, raging but not speechless. In fact, he was most articulate. I said I would see what I could do, but when I phoned him back, it was to say that we could get another spear made, but even airmail, less predictable then than it is now, would not get it to the other end on time. "What will you be doing?" he asked me.

"Waiting around for the spear and then—"

"Why don't you bring it out yourself? Wouldn't you like to come to the opening?"

So I flew to Chicago the following night, with mountains of my own luggage and a sewing machine just in case, and the spear held carefully in my hand. I checked in at the Ambassador East as Jack's guest and had a ball for three days, the most expensive spear carrier I know of.

Everything Jack liked in costuming was expensive, particularly the beading, which had to be done by hand. On all the

Hindoo costumes he used beads where the originals might
have had embroidery. The beads caught nightclub lights better. Once we found a good beading place, I think he would
have bought them out if he could have, and just kept them
working steadily for him. When Jack Cole finally did the
choreography for *Kismet* I am sure that the song, "Baubles,
Bangles, and Beads," was secretly dedicated to him.

After spending much of my designing time with people
who haggled over pennies, it was a pleasure to be associated
with someone who was interested in quality and workman-
ship. If the end result was going to be good enough, Jack
was willing to pay for it. But he surpassed even his own reputation for extravagance in the matter of "The Coat." He was
going into the Persian Room, and he intended to be as spectacular as the setting. All new costumes for everybody, and
for himself he wanted a tunic, much the shape of those
Nehru used to wear, made completely of Persian lamb. (This
was before mink became the thing to wear to a football game,
and Persian was still a top fur.) Yes, he wanted real Persian,
and moreover, it was to be embroidered. . . . So we went
shopping at the furrier's, and thank heaven I had him along,
because where I would have settled for some perfectly nice
skins that I would have happily worn on the street, he found
a bundle that were softer, blacker, and with a marvelous
"bean" at a little over twice what I would have dared pay.
I made a canvas, fitted it, and sent it to the furrier. As the
pieces were finished they went off to be embroidered all over
before being sewed together.

It was a gorgeous coat. The body was covered all over
with gold embroidery in a scroll design. The sleeves, which

came out separately and free from the shoulders, were of black suede, solidly embroidered and jeweled. There were a few jewels down the front, little things like the Star of India, and then the whole thing was lined in pure silk taffeta—red. I took one look, gasped with delight over the finished product, and insisted on an insurance policy.

The audience gasped too when Jack and dancers made their entrance on opening night. One very illustrious-looking lady with a lorgnette and a ringside seat couldn't take her eyes off what was going on on the floor. She never moved that eyepiece off Jack, not his face, or his hands or feet, but about the upper middle torso. Finally, when he got close enough, she reached out a hand and patted him soundly on the der-riere. Then she sank, and that is the only word for it, back. And in a stage whisper that could have been heard backstage, she confided to her husband, "My God, Henry, it's *real!*"

Another bracket that might be interesting is the one- or two-man show, and can include everything from a lady lecturer to a two-piano team. You can end up with a pair of actors or a lady cellist. For the concert stage, you do not need the musi-cal knowledge recommended for ballet work; what you need is to have watched the performer through at least one ap-pearance. You are trying to find out what the professional movements are, and what portion of the performer's body is presented to the audience. Of course, we are talking about women, now. Men in this category are usually in white tie.

If you are designing for a lady pianist, you will notice that, as with a dance frock, the back of the dress is very im-portant. That is what the audience will see most. Also she will need a skirt that arranges easily on a piano bench, foot freedom for the pedal, and if her arms are unattractive, a dress designed so that long sleeves are part of the design and do not look like tacked-on appendages. If you must have something of this nature, be aggressive about the requirement, never let it look like an afterthought. The lady cellist, on the other hand, has to have the very full skirt, and the back of her dress is hardly seen.

To find out what a lecturing lady should wear, look at her audience. Get their *status* status. Then dress her in the same genre but quietly better than the women she will talk to. She must never arouse envy. You only want the group who have hired her to *like* her. That crazy hat would make women loathe her on sight, unless she were a millinery creator and she did it deliberately. People didn't *love* Hedda Hopper because of her headgear. She had power, and that gave her power to get away with wearing what she pleased. She was just indulging her own fondness for hats, not considering what was good for a public appearance.

I know this area well, having spent a year and a half doing about four or five lectures a week, in everything from a large living room to very large civic auditoriums. I think I have lectured in everything but a church and have had plenty of time to find out what was successful and what was not, and to analyze why. Let's begin at the top.

A hat is not required, unless most of the women in the audience wear them. If they do, and the lecturer is going to, be sure it is a becoming one rather than crazy. It should not have a brim that shades the face. Most monologists use their faces, and it will only infuriate an audience not to be able to see their expressions.

Proceeding to the dress, find out when your lecturer delivers her speeches. Many of these busy women work a twenty-four hour shift, not all in one day, of course. But she may have to appear morning, noon, and night, which means she will have to carry along a wardrobe for an early appearance, luncheon clothes, late day, and formal evening wear. This need not mean as many dresses as you might think, because since she is always changing her audience, she need not change her clothes so often, except for her own personal pleasure. Many women hate to wear the same outfit twice in a row. Others like to assemble one costume and then wear it until it has to go to the cleaners. Check this preference. Also allow for that cleaning and remember there must be a full substitute.

Shoes comfortable, not too high-heeled unless your woman is very short, and trim. Simple, not distracting. As to the accessories, I am against that touch of white at the throat and wrists unless it is so detachable the dress can be worn without it. Otherwise your lady becomes a slave to the washbasin, the traveling iron, and a needle and some thread she is always misplacing. If she wants her white, for heaven's sake make it so it snaps in and out.

Gloves are very important, but keep them classic and easy to care for. Remember that most of her audience will be of the older generation, probably, and many of the Ladies' Clubs of America are composed of members who were brought up to believe that no lady ever appeared on the street with naked hands. That would be indecent exposure. Also, the gloves can have a function other than as a character testimonial. Ida Bailey Allen, one of the great cookbook authorities, used to give cooking demonstrations to which she always wore gloves a button or two longer than absolutely required, which meant they *showed*. She kept them on until she was behind the range or counter at which she was going to work. When the audience had begun to wonder if she was going to sift the flour in gloved hands she would appear to remember them and take them off to be tucked in an apron pocket, making some small joke about it. She said this dissipated stiffness in the group.

I can't say I agree with Emily Kimbrough about not wearing jewelry. I like it, if it is right for the background of the dress. I don't mean outrageous costume jewelry, such as jangling chandelier earrings that are distracting, but if simple button earrings suit you, wear them, say I. An interesting piece of adornment, and I do not mean a Kohinoor diamond, is always a good conversational gambit. I have too-long arms, so when in short sleeves I always wore two Whitby jet bracelets that had belonged to my grandmother. You would be surprised at how many of the women I sat next to at dinners or luncheons were interested in those unusually shaped armbands. They were strung on steel wires that were actually old watch springs, and as icebreakers, were pure gold.

Check the potential weather, and be sure your lady lecturer is equipped with storm boots or parkas if she goes into that kind of territory. And, lastly, consider her coat. I say lastly, since it is good to establish what it is going over, and the color schemes it must envelop. Keep these to a minimum, by the way, for the sake of shoes and bags. For coats, mink is always nice, and goes with everything. So does seal or beaver. If her budget doesn't run to pelts, or she is speaking for the

Antivivisectionists, or the ASPCA, design her a universal coat, one that will be equally good over a suit or an evening dress. While you are at it, make it full enough to curl up under in a waiting room or on a train, as she will learn to catch forty winks whenever she can, and it is not often convenient to carry a blanket.

Last category is the diseuse or monologist or solo singer. For the singer, go back and reread the rules for the lady lecturer—then break almost every one of them. For one thing, she is supposed to be very high-style and chic. Half her audience is apt to be as interested in her looks as in her voice. Let her wear any shoe height she wishes that she can perform in and that gives her body the best proportions. She will probably be alone on the stage, with no introducing chairwoman as a figure contrast. Make her as attractive as possible, here a little envy is not a dangerous thing—it will simply add revenue. If she is not pretty, do what you can with hair styling, and allow her all the makeup that will contribute to her looks. Above all, she must be dramatic. Jewels, furs, the Taj Mahal's the limit as long as your girl's got the personality to stand up to it. Be sure to keep her as pretty as possible. The idea is that she may be stunning, but never ludicrous. Anything that might elicit a snicker is *out*. If she is the most sensational thing on view that evening, for the right reasons, you've done a good job. She is supposed to be.

For this, I still believe in simple clothes, but striking. Black and white is one of the most reliable schemes, or a flame of red. Unless she has some particular coloring herself that makes peacock blue an absolute must, stay away from trick colors, and don't forget to check what her background will be—a set, or simple black curtains?

The category of mimes and diseuses includes a wide variety, from Ruth Draper to Cornelia Otis Skinner. The recently fashionable "readings" including drama, poetry, and the *Pickwick Papers* come under this heading as far as costume is concerned. And except for the occasional one-man Broadway shows, such as *An Evening with Bea Lillie,* they are generally set on the same smaller stages that serve the lady lecturer.

If, for example, you were doing costumes for the incomparable Miss Lillie for one of her solo performances, you would have a very special case. Although the program may announce that Lady Peel will appear as a woman shopper, or a stage star backstage, or a maid trying on her absent mistress's clothes, or even Madame Butterfly, she is always being herself. She does not really pretend to be anything but the famous Bea, and her costumes are never intended to disguise. They are not meant to submerge or hide the actress, but to enhance her and make her sparkle. Many years ago I made one outfit for her, for street wear, and during the fittings I got brave enough to ask her who did her costumes. "I do them myself," was the answer, and it was quite likely true. Certainly she has sheer genius for selecting props for herself, whether it is a string of beads or a moth-eaten boa. For when she wants to look elegant, a famous Frenchman does her clothes, with, I would bet, a personal assist from the subject herself, who certainly manages to look right, which means look herself, whenever she appears.

But since Miss Lillie is in a class by herself, you are not

apt to run into the problem of dressing her or someone like her. There aren't enough of her sort to go round.

The more familiar brand of diseuse is the one who comes out in a little rag, throws a shawl over her head, and instantly becomes a hungry child or your mother's next-door neighbor. But though I have called her costume an old rag, that is not what it should be. It should be the Universal Dress, all things to all people, and if it fails of this it is nothing.

Several years ago I did the costumes for an act—I don't know what else to call it—called *Two's a Company*. The two were Edith Atwater and Albert Dekker, and they ran a gamut from *Macbeth* to a satire on *Macbeth* with poetry and comic sketches along the way. Albert wore a dark suit, or dinner clothes, but Edie's requirements included morning, cocktail, and evening things, modern and fashionable enough so that they would serve for the luncheon, dinner, or after-theatre party as well as the stage. She used some props, but very few —a rose, a fan, a shawl, a hooded cape. Each dress, when seen with the accompanying accessory, had to look as if that particular moment in its life was what it had been designed for. We had to avoid excess, since there was a baggage problem as they flew everywhere. She had a beautiful coat, a voluminous natural cashmere with a large cape collar, that reversed to show its white wool lining and become an evening wrap. Under this went a tweedy suit to travel in.

As the tour went on, she settled into the three dresses that worked best and mailed the others home. One was black velvet, absolutely untrimmed, street length, and the only thing it did was to make no bones about the beautiful figure underneath. When she wanted to hide that shape, she wrapped a paisley shawl around herself, sometimes over the shoulders, sometimes over her head. The second dress was a black and white pique that looked as if it had been embroidered, a Swiss import that was worth its weight on the luggage scales since it fascinated the women of her audiences, who all wanted to get close to it. Besides, it was washable.

The last dress was the best of all and most useful. Black wool jersey from throat to floor, it curved up at the side of the neck and plunged to a narrow but deep V. The sleeves were long, and fitted the arm naturally, ending in points that came down onto the hands. The body of the dress conformed to the body until below the knees it fell into folds so full they looked like the flutings of a column. It had both movement and life, and yet could be absolutely still when the wearer wanted to project repose.

I knew these dresses were good because they saw a lot of service. They were brought to me for repairs as long as that was possible, and finally duplicated rather than replaced. Trying to analyze what was good about them, this is what I come up with: They were simple, lovely, dignified dresses on their own, and all becoming. They *fitted*. Worn with the proper accessories, they had enough style to appear like ordinary social clothing. But on the stage they were transmutable into the outer cover for any part Edith wanted to play. Except for the pique, which was used only for the lighter programs, they were suitable for *John Brown's Body* or *Macbeth*. They were foils for an apron for a scene from *Our Town;* she could cradle a baby—a rolled scarf—for the *Harpweaver,* or tie the same scarf over her head for an Ellis Island immigrant, or flutter it from her hand in a dizzy impersonation of a torch singer. In all these characterizations, the clothes became foils or backgrounds, while the important thing was the actress and what she was doing. They were never obtrusive, and I doubt if anyone in the audience could have described them to you at the end of the evening, but they were not nonentities. It is hard to put into words what these costumes should do and look like. I suppose, thinking it over, they are among the most difficult and most rewarding things I have worked on.

That's once very lightly over the field. Not enough to ensure you will come up with the first prize, but at least to give a clue as to where to look in this treasure hunt. I do not pretend to have left no stone unturned, only to suggest where to look. Police the area that is most appealing, and you may come up with an idea of your own. After all, there is no niche more comfortable, and no position more satisfactory than the one in which you have written the job description to suit yourself, after a good long look in the mirror.

18

The
Temperamental Requirements

Up to this point we have been trying to follow along the uneven path of a Broadway production, with occasional digressive steps off that anything-but-straight-and-narrow to allow the author to step up on some personal soapboxes and to explore some non-Broadway alternate routes. An attempt has been made to show you what the job of designing costumes for the theatre would be like. Now I think it is time to consider whether you, personally, would like the job, and, frankly, whether it would like you.

To be a success at it, there are certain personal characteristics the theatrical designer should have. Lacking these does not mean that you will have to give up your preoccupation with clothes—it simply means that you should operate in another area. After all, Seventh Avenue is the street that runs next to Broadway.

To begin with, I think you *must* be stagestruck. Through and through, you should be as dedicated to the theatre as if you were an actor, a director, a playwright. You should believe, for instance, that a good play is more exciting than a good book, in spite of the fact that it will have a more limited audience. The fact that it is alive should count with you, as opposed to its being just printed words on a page. A really fine actor or actress should seem more important and newsworthy to you than a successful businessman, and the dedicated producer should be a larger figure in your opinion than the head of an advertising agency or a department store. Given the choice between a meal ticket and one for the Morosco or Music Box, you should unhesitatingly choose the latter. Take your temperature, using this scale to see how feverish you are, and if the answer is "yes" in all departments, you have got the disease, and it is probably too late for inoculation.

Because if you don't start with this virus in your system you will never survive the miasmic atmosphere of Broadway and the theatre. It will soon begin to seem unreasonable and irrational, phony and extravagant to you. The people you are dealing with will appear to be egomaniacal, the pace impossible, and the rewards trivial compared to the effort you expend. There is no question but that you could earn more money working at another profession. The question is—would you have half as good a time?

But, if you have been born stagestruck, you will see stars.

Aside from this primary characteristic, what else will you need? For one thing, vitality or energy, and the physical stamina to support. Give up all ideas of a thirty-five-hour workweek. If you can get it done in forty you are either very lucky or have an organizational ability that is close to genius. You will be up in the morning while the people you are relating to are still asleep, and in the final weeks, at least, you will probably start additional work when they retire. Your meals will be irregular and often bad; your hair, doctor, and dentist appointments must frequently be foregone, and the only time you will have time to look after your own wardrobe and be well dressed yourself will be when you are out of work. And all this will be because the day is just not long enough, once you have that job to do.

This kind of existence separates you from such friends as you have who lead so-called normal lives. While you are working they will have to meet you for lunch near the shoe place, or the wigmaker's, or in the rehearsal area. You will become an undependable dinner guest, and may very well have to miss your own birthday party. Christmas? You can depend on its finding you in New Haven or Bridgeport, with all your packages still unwrapped, perhaps unpurchased. Are these things important to you?

Have you patience and the fortitude to smile at calamity? Patience is an essential—you can never take "no" for an answer, or give it. There will be things that will have to be done over and over again, until they are exactly right. Even, sometimes, when it is not your idea of right, but you have been overruled by a majority that includes actor, director, set designer. You can never say, "It's too much trouble." You will just have to take that trouble, nicely and without grumbling.

You should have a passion for a certain sort of exactitude yourself, for getting things right. This will show up in the completed picture as one of your assets, and it will make easier the hammering at your suppliers that is so often necessary. Even Brooks Costume may try to convince you that you don't really need lace on the collar *and* cuffs, since *they* have only ordered enough for one of these places. And almost right in the shoe shade that is supposed to match the dress isn't right enough. It won't do, and must be done over again.

Another one of the secondary characteristics you must consider about yourself is your attitude toward money. How really important is this commodity in your idea of your future life? The costume designer needs a certain ambivalence about it. For one thing, this career is no guaranteed road to riches. I do not mean to say that people in the theatre do not acquire wealth. There have been some cozy, comfortable fortunes made here, to be sure. But what you must realize is that these are the exceptions, which is why they are talked about. They are so far from the rule that the figures, if they were available, would shock you. Not for want of talent, and not for want of trying, but there just aren't enough jobs to go round. Ask the Actors' Fund, for instance. It's the irregular verb to eat.

The other side of the coin—while the costume designer must maintain a dashing indifference to wealth or possibly even financial security for *himself*, he must at all times treat the producer's dollar as if it were the last in the world. His heart and soul must not only be in creating a superb production but he usually has to fight and die for the money to do it with. And the accounting that shows where every penny fell by the wayside must be turned in with the exactitude of a CPA, usually in triplicate. So if the prospective designer has a slight schizoid tendency, here is where to put it to good use.

Another useful mental aberration would be to *like* job-hunting. It takes, as I figure it, about four productions a year to keep both your appetite and your bank manager placated. So, for the first few years at least, before you get to the established position when the job comes hunting for you, you will have to put yourself in the degrading, ignominious position of chasing employment. You cannot afford to live an ivory tower personal life. You must be as extrovert and outgoing, pushy, even, as any actor. But with this added disadvantage—where on the hit or miss basis by which the actor's life is run, he may occasionally land that hit that will keep him off the slave block for a year or so, the costume designer is practically out of work after the curtain has gone up on the Broadway opening. This is true even if the opening is a *My Fair Lady*, since very few costume designers get a percentage of the show.

While it is perfectly true that having a *Fair Lady* to your credit makes the next step easier, stop and count on your fingers the outstanding smashes of that caliber there are a year, and then find out what the odds are on your getting that job by checking with the union to see how many members in good standing are at that moment unemployed.

And then, of course, you will need a certain amount of Opening Night Phobia. Or should it be called Opening Nightitus? At any rate it is a fairly serious disease that is prevalent in the Broadway area. If you haven't got it, or don't catch at least a mild infection from your associates, you may still make it in the theatre, but there is no question but that you will be laboring under a handicap. Fortunately the period of infection is short. It is really like the twenty-four-hour virus.

Unless you are so provident as to have already attended to this, you will wake up the morning of the opening with the happy realization that you have to send telegrams for that evening's performance. To everybody. It will never do just to send them to your favorites, or even to the people with whom you have become friendly. Unless you wire everyone, down to the last walk-on's understudy, the next local affliction to break out will be a rash of hurt feelings, very infectious.

You can, if your calligraphy is legible enough, do little handwritten notes, but this is even more of a strain. And if you want to try cheating, you can send one telegram to the entire company that may or may not make the bulletin board backstage, and where it will get about the same amount of attention as that old menu from the sandwich stand across the street that has been there since the play before the last started rehearsals. But this is actually the coward's way.

And the terrible part is that you must be funny. Not once, but differently funny for each and every person on that list. If you can squeeze sincerity in, or incorporate affection too, fine. But these are really nonessential. The joke has to be there, just as surely as if you were one of the writers on the Bob Hope show, and if you can make it a belly laugh instead of just a chuckle, it will increase your status as a designer.

Often the fount of all this wit and humor is the title of the play, and sometimes this does give you an assist. But when you consider that all the non-privy-to-the-script friends of the actors who are also sending wires have nothing else to go on, you can figure on a certain amount of competition. And as it says in the contest rules, "In case of duplication, the entry bearing the earliest postmark . . ."

There have been some rather glorious telegrams based on titles. My favorite goes back to the thirties, for the opening of a Paul Osborn play called simply *Oliver Oliver*. I was worrying that bone pretty hard when Mildred Dunnock came up with this lovely to our mutual friend. Just ten words, notice. WISHING WISHING YOU YOU SUCCESS SUCCESS IN IN OLIVER OLIVER.

Here are a few nontitular telegrams: The first is sort of going the rounds right now. IF YOU CAN'T LAY THEM IN THE AISLES, TAKE THEM HOME.

These last are of the "in" variety: First, for an unknown young actor making a first Broadway appearance, from that very witty man, Eric Rhodes—OF COURSE I KNEW HIM BEFORE HE BECAME SO TREMENDOUSLY SUCCESSFUL. And, finally, to an actor who was involved in about six scenes of a play, but only as a walk-on, from his wife—WELL DON'T JUST STAND THERE SAY SOMETHING. Or for the opening of *Big Fish, Little Fish*—ONE MAN'S MEAT IS ANOTHER MAN'S POISSON.

If it is a good-sized company, this telegraphic approach to opening night will, with your other working chores, take you up to curtain time and possibly even cause you to slip into that aisle seat late enough to make your neighbors frown. But the worst part, for me at least, is still ahead. It begins when the final curtain goes down, and can be called, for want of better, more heart-rending words, that Compulsory Visit to Everyone's Dressing Room.

If you are glib about the white, or social, lie, this may not be as painful for you as it is to others. Personally, I can skinny out of the unwanted dinner invitation or the tickets to the dull lecture with a fair approximation of ease. I can lie like an adman with a new sponsor about something I know nothing about. It is when my critical faculties, in relationship to my work, are concerned that I begin to stammer if I cannot blurt out the truth.

In wait for you backstage, dressing-room doors open so you can't sneak past, will be every blessed member of that perhaps unblessed company. And somewhere, holding the hand of one of the performers, you will encounter the author, the director, and the producer. Custom demands that you make your "devoirs" to each of these people, and they are all going to look at you, as you come up to them, with "Well, what did you think?" written in headlines on their faces. And, well, what did you think? Nine times out of ten you can't say it.

With the fall of that first-night curtain it is obligatory that you make your way backstage and knock on every dressing-room door. It is still too soon to know the real reception of the play. A first-night audience is so packed with friends and backers that their encouraging applause has to be discounted. This is, except for the critics, a claque—not a true sample of the public. And so, until the reviews come out, you are going to have to suffice. You will be asked, "What do you think?" as seriously as if you had eyes that could read through the skulls of those men who sit on the aisles and try to leave the theatre with impassive faces that give no hint of what they are about to start writing. If you have always wanted to be a play critic, here is your brief chance. But take along your waterwings—it's deep water back there.

Even if you haven't the foggiest idea whether you have just seen the next Pulitzer-prize play, people with the next winners of the Tony awards, or the worst turkey that should have been left in some disconnected icebox, you are going to have to say *something*. Best idea is to stick to the costumes, as subject matter, or some enthusiastic comment on personal appearance, with a "You were wonderful!" thrown in to keep the beat. Unless, of course, you really have a genuine, constructive opinion to offer. If, through ten or twelve dressing rooms, after weeks of having your mind prodded already, you really do, well—you're just lucky, I guess.

Or born to the theatre. Because this opening-night personality is a distinct asset that won't do your work for you, but does come in handily at the end of it. And since the backstage appearance is practically *de rigueur,* you can see why I list a facility with its language and customs as part of the temperamental requirements for the profession of costume designer. There have been people, of course, who don't even go to the opening. But if you have that first qualification, that of being stagestruck, how can you stay away?

50520

PN
2067
V6

VOLLAND, VIRGINIA
    DESIGNING WOMAN.

DATE DUE

GAYLORD   PRINTED IN U.S.A.